Making Connections

with Mathematics

Making Connections
with Mathematics

Authors

John Egsgard
Gary Flewelling
Craig Newell
Wendy Warburton

Editorial Advisers

Wendy Warburton
Peter Wright

Janson Publications, Inc. Providence, Rhode Island

Photo Credits and Acknowledgments: Alberta Government Audio Visual Services, p. 11; Bryn Mawr College Archives, p. 32; Courtesy of Professor Coxeter, p. 28; Thomas Fisher Rare Book Library, University of Toronto, p. 25; Courtesy of IBM Corporation, p. 22; Lowell Observatory, p. 91; NASA p. 89; National Radio Astronomy Observatory, operated by Associated Universities, Inc., under contract with the National Science Foundation, p. 81; and Bertrand Russell Archives, McMaster University, p. 27.

Originally published as part of **MATHEMATICS: A Search for Meaning**, Copyright ©1987, Gage Educational Publishing Company, a divison of Canada Publishing Corporation.

98 97 96 95 94 93 92 91 90 89 88 8 7 6 5 4 3 2 1

ISBN: 0-939765-27-6

Contents

vii **Mathematical Content Index**

ix **Symbols and Abbreviations**

x **To The Teacher**

1 **The Arts**

2 Connection 1: Music and Transformations

5 Connection 2: Choreography

9 **Biology**

10 Connection 3: Human Growth

11 Connection 4: Sampling in Nature and Industry

14 Connection 5: Symmetry in Nature

15 Connection 6: Paleontology and Genealogy

18 Connection 7: The Human Body and Exponential Functions

21 **Biographies**

22 Connection 8: Ada Byron Lovelace – The First Computer Programmer

23 Connection 9: Eratosthenes (c. 276 B.C. – c. 194 B.C.)

25 Connection 10: Descartes

26 Connection 11: Bertrand Russell

28 Connection 12: H.S.M. Coxeter

30 Connection 13: Sonya Kovalevskaya

32 Connection 14: Emmy Noether

33 **Business**

34 Connection 15: Probability in Insurance

36 Connection 16: Linear Programming

39 Connection 17: May I Have Your Opinion

41 **Computers**

42 Connection 18: Revolutions

44 Connection 19: Flight Simulation

47 Connection 20: Secret Codes and Large Primes

50 Connection 21: Information, Please

53 Connection 22: Game Theory

55 **Earth Science**

56 Connection 23: Mathematical Models

58 Connection 24: Math Models – The Greenhouse Effect
60 Connection 25: Tides
62 Connection 26: Waves
64 Connection 27: Food Needs and World Resources
67 Engineering
68 Connection 28: Ratios for a Reason
70 Connection 29: Working with Formulas
72 Connection 30: Construction Electrician
73 Connection 31: Trigonometry in Design and Construction
75 Space
76 Connection 32: The Motion of a Free Fall
77 Connection 33: Distortion
78 Connection 34: Black Holes
80 Connection 35: Telescopes
83 Connection 36: Physics and the Geometry of the Universe
86 Connection 37: Non-Euclidean Geometries
89 Connection 38: Measurements in Space
91 Connection 39: Comets (The Cosmic Pinball Machine)
93 Annotated Bibliography
97 Selected Answers

Mathematical Content Index

Algebra

Formulas Connection 26: Waves, p. 62; Connection 29: Working with Formulas, p. 70; Connection 30: Construction Electrician, p. 72; Connection 32: The Motion of a Free Fall, p. 76; Connection 34: Black Holes, p. 78.

Ratio and Proportion Connection 6: Paleontology and Geneology, p. 15; Connection 23: Mathematical Models, p. 56; Connection 24: Mathematical Models – the Greenhouse Effect, p. 58; Connection 27: Food Needs and World Resources, p. 64; Connection 28: Ratios for a Reason, p. 68.

Structure Connection 14: Emmy Noether, p. 32.

Analytic Geometry

Connection 10: Descartes, p. 25; Connection 16: Linear Programming, p. 36; Connection 35: Telescopes, p. 80; Connection 39: Comets, p. 91.

Computer Science

Connection 8: Ada Byron Lovelace, p. 22; Connection 10: Descartes, p. 25; Connection 18: Revolutions, p. 42; Connection 19: Flight Simulation, p. 44; Connection 38: Measurements in Space, p. 89.

Geometry

Plane geometry Connection 5: Symmetry in Nature, p. 14; Connection 9: Eratosthenes, p. 23; Connection 33: Distortion, p. 77.

Other geometries Connection 1: Music and Transformations, p. 2; Connection 12: H.S.M. Coxeter, p. 28; Connection 36: Physics and the Geometry of the Universe, p. 83; Connection 37: Non-Euclidean Geometries, p. 86.

Modern Mathematics

Notation Connection 2: Choreography, p. 5.

Set Theory Connection 11: Bertrand Russell, p. 26.

Information Theory Connection 21: Information, Please, p. 50.

Game Theory Connection 22: Game Theory, p. 53.

Number Theory

Connection 13: Sonya Kovalevskaya, p. 30; Connection 20: Secret Codes and Large Primes, p. 47.

Probability and Statistics

Connection 6: Paleontology and Geneology, p. 15; Connection 15: Probability in Insurance, p. 34; Connection 17: May I Have Your Opinion, p. 39; Connection 23: Mathematical Models, p. 56; Connection 24: Math Models – the Greenhouse Effect, p. 58; Connection 27: Food Needs and World Resources, p. 64.

Trigonometry

Connection 25: Tides, p. 60; Connection 31: Trigonometry in Design and Construction, p. 73.

Symbols and Abbreviations

A	amperes
a	acceleration
cm	centimeter
CO_2	carbon dioxide
°C	degrees Celsius
G	gravitational constant
g	acceleration due to gravity, 9.8 m/s^2
g	grams
h	hours
I	current
kg	kilogram
km	kilometer
P	power
R	resistance
s	second
W	watts
∠	angle
°	degrees
Ω	ohms
△	triangle

To The Teacher

The lessons in MAKING CONNECTIONS: WITH MATHEMATICS are designed to encourage students to think about many aspects of mathematics—as a tool for the sciences and as a human enterprise. The organizaion of the lessons into subject areas such as business or the arts, allows you to emphasize particular applications and capitalize on and develop individual student interests.

The activities themselves involve a range of mathematical skills. The Mathematical Content Index will provide guidance in deciding which Connections may be most appropriate for your class. Within each lesson you may find that some of the activities are more appropriate than others for your class. The lessons can be viewed as starting points. They may lead to more questions and encourage further investigation along lines which interest the individual student or class. Flexibility and adaptability are important features of the material.

Two other features of the book are a list of symbols for easy reference and an annotated bibliography. The bibliography can be used by students as a guide to further exploration of topics presented in the lessons or to familiarize yourself with topics that are new to you.

Please note that when an activity suggests contacting a person in a specific occupation for information, such as a wild-life officer, local circumstances may make this difficult or impossible. You are encouraged to modify the exercise by calling on your own experience or the expertise of your students, their parents, or other members of the community.

Many of the lessons provide opportunities for students to research and write about the topics presented. This feature increases the usefulness of the lessons for math club projects, enrichment activities, extra credit, or class projects. Most importantly, the activities highlight the role of mathematics in the world around us and provide opportunities for students to use their mathematical skills together with other talents and interests.

The Arts

Connection 1 Music and Transformations

The way that relations are graphed can be compared to the way that music is written. Music is written on sets of five horizontal lines called staves. The horizontal position of a note represents the time when the note begins. The vertical position of a note represents the pitch of the note. This method of recording notes is similar to using x and y-axes to graph a relation in mathematics.

Time on horizontal axis and pitch on vertical axis.

The study of relations involves several types of **transformations**. We will consider the ways in which transformations similar to translations, reflections, compressions, and dilatations affect music. Recall that a **translation** is a change in position of a figure in which the shape and size of the figure remain the same. In a **reflection**, the original figure and its image are reversed. Additionally, all segments joining corresponding points on the original figure and its image have a common perpendicular bisector. Both of these transformations result in images that are congruent to the original figure. A **dilatation**, on the other hand, produces a reduction or enlargement of the original figure. It involves a change in position and size but not in shape. Thus, the figure and its image are similar. Finally, a **compression** is a reduction in the horizontal or vertical extent of the figure.

Now, let us compare each of these transformations to a similar change in music:

A horizontal translation corresponds to a change in the starting time of a piece of music. In music, this change is exemplified by a round or a canon. For example, one group might begin singing "Campfires Burning," then another group begins, and then another. All of the groups singing the same tune at different times form multi-part harmonies.

Same tune, same pitch, played at different times. (Horizontal shift.)

A vertical translation corresponds to a change in the pitch of a piece of music. For example, when a young girl and her father sing "O Canada" together, they begin singing the same tune at the same time, but at different pitches. In many pieces of music the same theme recurs at a different time and at a different pitch, which is similar to both a horizontal and vertical translation. This technique is used to magnificent effect in the great organ fugues of Bach.

Same tune, different pitches, played at the same time. (Vertical shift.)

A reflection in the x-axis corresponds to an inversion in music. An interval that was rising in an original theme is descending in the inversion. However, a vertical reflection corresponds to the notes of a theme being played in reverse order.

(Inversion, reflection in horizontal axis.)

for ev - er and

for ev - er and

Horizontal compressions and stretches correspond to a theme being repeated faster and slower respectively, while vertical stretches and compressions correspond to the intervals between notes being augmented or diminished.

(Horizontal stretch.)

Hal - le - lu - jah! Hal - le - lu - jah!

(Vertical stretch and shift.)

ev - er. Hal-le-lu - jah!

ev - er. Hal-le-lu - jah!

Other transformations occur when a theme is elaborated by the addition of other notes between the notes of the original theme. This is equivalent to the elaboration of the equilateral triangle into the geometric shape known as the snowflake curve, shown below.

Elaboration of theme by addition of extra notes.

The snowflake curve is generated by dividing each side of the original triangle into three equal parts, constructing an equilateral triangle on each of the middle thirds (*Step 1*), and then deleting the base of each new triangle (*Step 2*). The process is repeated on each exterior side of the figure as many times as desired to produce the snowflake curve (*Step 3*).

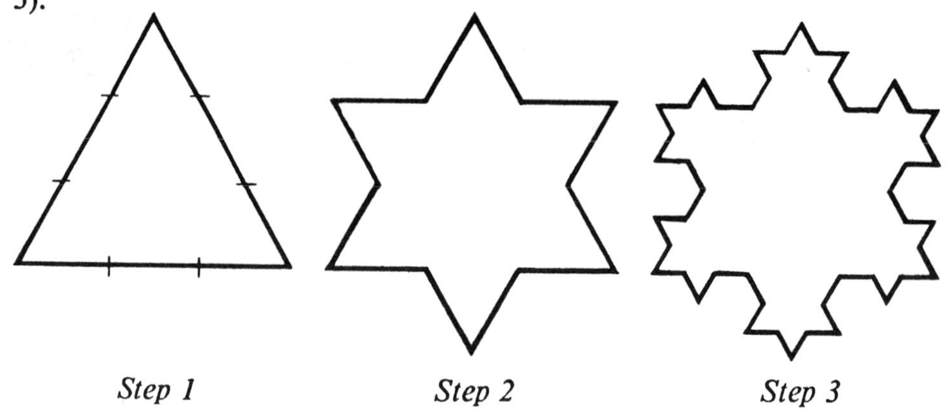

Step 1 *Step 2* *Step 3*

The "Hallelujah Chorus" in Handel's *Messiah* is used to provide the last four musical examples above. In this piece of music the single phrase "Hallelujah" is repeated very many times and in very many forms. These transformations of musical theme are used in all types of music, classical and popular. It is the recognition of the same theme recurring in different forms that gives us pleasure in whatever type of music we enjoy.

Explorations

1. Look at several of Bach's fugues from *The Well-Tempered Clavier*, Bach's collection of 48 preludes and fugues written in each major and minor key. You might want to start with Fugue II for three voices, BWV 847. (BWV stands for Bach-Werke-Verzeichnis, a thematic cataloguing of Bach's work.) The theme is introduced in the first two measures. See if you can find repetitions of the theme in all three of ethe voices. Where is the theme inverted? Does it start at different pitches, that is, different vertical translations?

2. Choose a current rock song and describe orally or in writing any examples of transformations that you find.

3. On a blank music staff make up a simple short tune. Then try inverting it and translating it in various ways. Play it on a piano or other instrument to see what it sounds like. Try playing the inverted and translated parts together. Describe how the combination sounds.

Connection 2 Choreography

A picture is worth a thousand words is an old, but true, saying. In many areas of life, graphs are used to *picture* information. For example, over many years choreographers have been developing a system of notation to describe the position of various parts of a dancer's body during a ballet. This development has been very difficult because there are so many variables involved. The position of each joint of the body needs to be designated in three-dimensional space.

Two main forms of notation are in common use today. They are Laban notation and Benesh notation, which was invented in 1947 by Rudolf Benesh. This notation is also used by physiotherapists and sports coaches to analyze and record the movements of patients and athletes respectively. In Benesh notation, the four quadrants of the Cartesian plane are used to represent the four limbs. (See figure 1.)

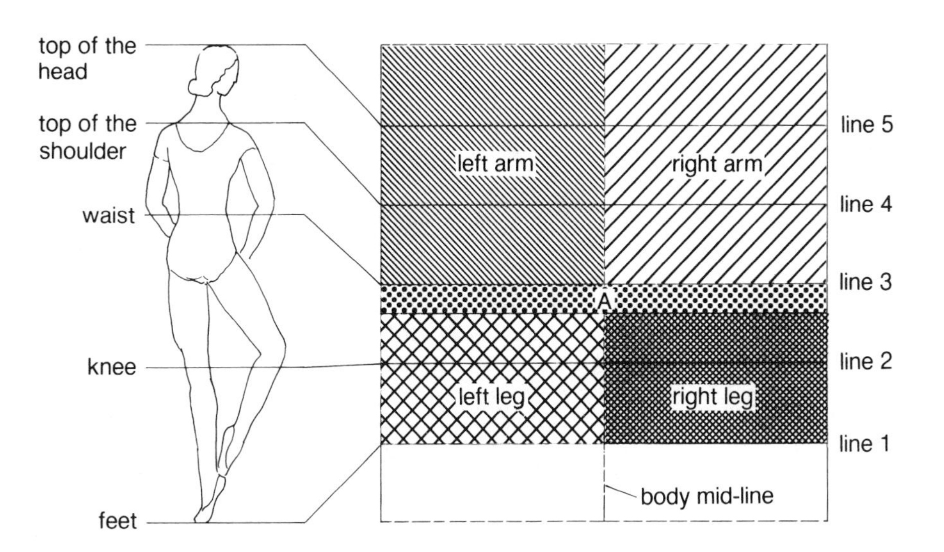

Figure 1
The shaded areas represent the domains of the body limbs. Region A represents the overlap between the top and bottom limb domains. Benesh score is written as observed from behind the dancer.

In Benesh notation, the angle of each limb, the torso, and the head is marked on a diagram. The position of each joint relative to the vertical plane (that is, in front of, level with, or behind the torso) is shown by the symbols in figure 2.

Figure 2

| in front (of the vertical plane) | — level (with the vertical plane) | • behind (the vertical plane) |

There are also symbols to show a limb crossing over from its usual quadrant to either the other side of the body (a lateral crossover), or above or below the waistline (a vertical crossover). (See figure 3.)

Figure 3

/ lateral crossover \ vertical crossover

Figure 4 shows a dancer's pose and the corresponding Benesh notation for the hands and feet.

Figure 4

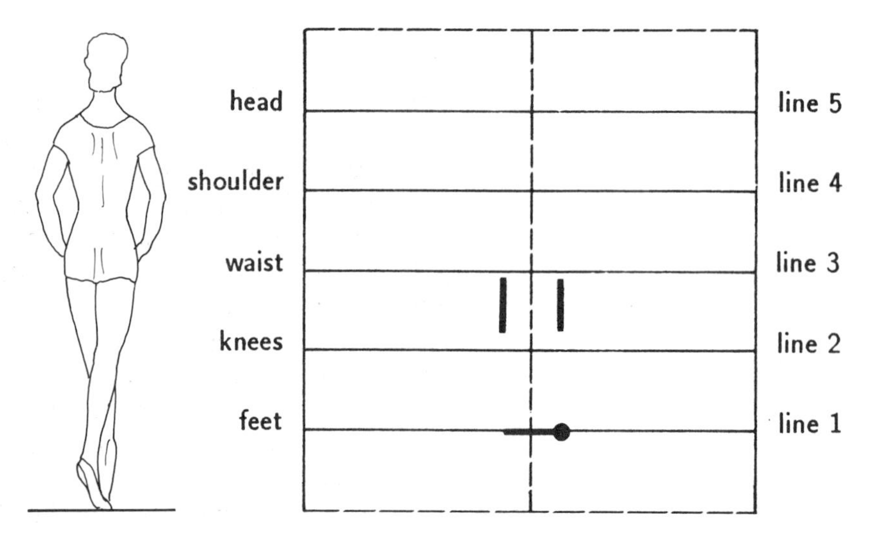

The notation shows that the right foot is behind the torso and the hands are below the waist.

Dancing is a motion and, therefore, a picture of one stationary position is not sufficient for a choreographer. A succession of these pictures must be used to display the movement of a dancer from one position to another.

Recording Benesh notation for all of the dancers in a ballet is a very tedious and error-prone task. A system of recording and editing Benesh notation on a computer has been developed at the University of Waterloo in Canada. Computerization has significantly speeded up the process and reduced the probability of error.

You may well be wondering why anyone would want to use such a complicated system of notation for dance when the movement can be recorded on film and video. Consider a similar situation with music. If you are learning to play a piece of music, it is often useful to hear a recording of another musician playing the same piece. However, that recording does not convey to you all of the details of the composer's original intentions, but it does add the interpretation of the particular musician who recorded the music. In order to learn a choreographer's original intentions, you need a choreographic score. This score needs to be written in a commonly uinderstood notation such as that developed by Benesh. The ballet can then be interpreted afresh by each different company of dancers.

Explorations

1. Think of a dancing pose and try to represent it in Benesh notation. Give your notation to a friend and ask him or her to strike the pose just from seeing your notation.
2. Record a series of three poses in Benesh notation to show movement. Again ask your friend to dance from your notes. What problems,

if any, did the dancer have? Ask a second friend to perform the movements. Describe any differences between the movements of the two dancers and suggest possible reasons for the differences.

3. Read about Laban notation or talk to a dance instructor about it. Compare and contrast Laban notation with Benesh notation. Decide which notation you feel is better and give reasons for your selection.

4. Ask a physiotherapist or a sports coach to show you how he or she uses Benesh notation. Write a report or give a demonstration based on your interview.

5. Read selections from a book about notation such as *A History of Mathematical Notation* by Floriani Cajori (Chicago: Open Court, 1928). How does notation develop? What do you feel are the characteristics of a good notation? Give examples from your reading.

6. Investigate the use of computers in choreography and/or in sports movement. Write a report or give a demonstration about your findings.

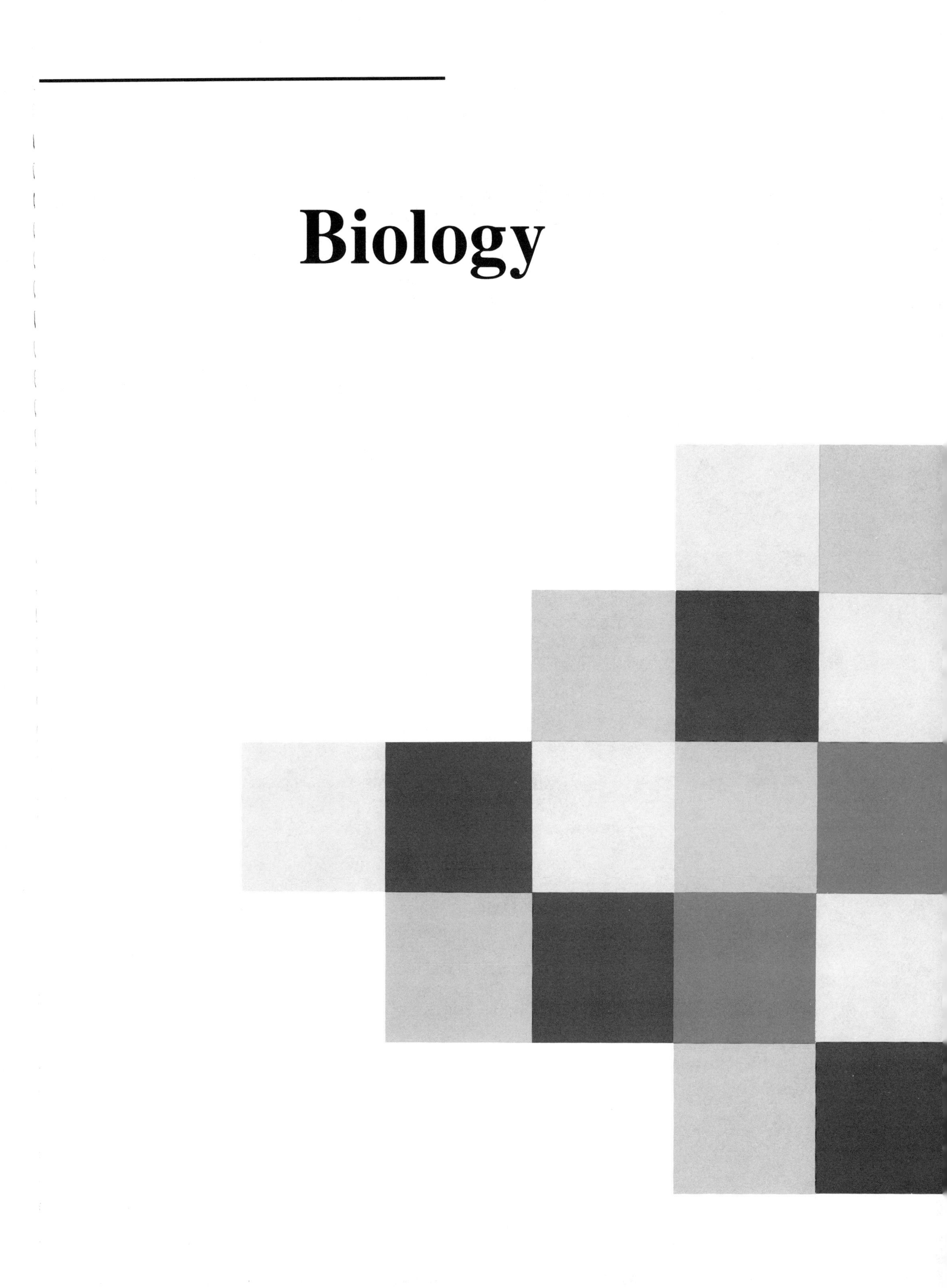
Biology

Connection 3 Human Growth

This graph illustrates average size for boys and girls at various ages. Notice that mass is indicated on the horizontal axis and height is on the vertical axis. Age in years, from 7 to 18, is marked at the appropriate points on each line. Look at the position of each age on the graph for girls and compare it to the position of the same age on the graph for boys. How do the growth patterns differ?

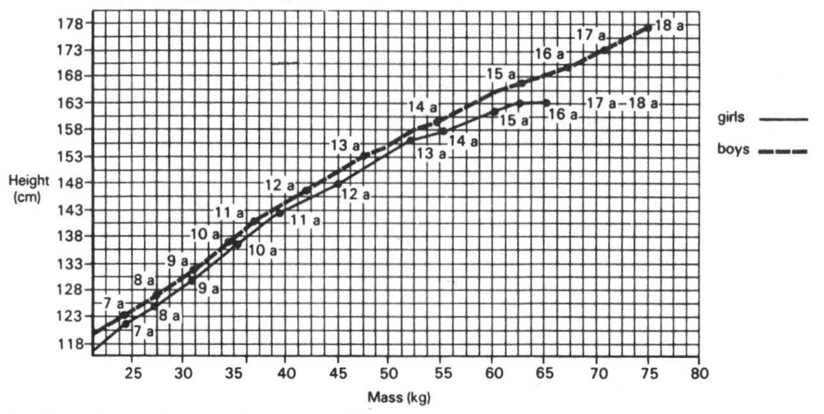

Notice that the points tend to spread at puberty and then appear closer together after a couple more years. What does this mean?

Suppose that the height of a male doubles between 2 years old and 20 years old, from 90 cm to 180 cm, and that his mass increases from 14 kg to 84 kg. In this case, his height has doubled, but his mass has increased by a factor of 6. If his height doubled again to 360 cm, and he continued to grow at the same rate, his mass would be 504 kg!

Explorations

1. Find out about average growth for babies from 0 to 2 years and create a graph like the one above. Compare growth during this period to growth at puberty.

2. What does it mean when the graph shown here has a slope of 1, that is, makes a 45° angle with each axis? What does it mean when the graph is nearly horizontal or nearly vertical?

3. Find out how the average sizes of humans have changed with time from the Bronze Age to Medieval times to the present. Graph your data and see if you can detect a pattern of change. Predict the average size of humans in 500 years.

4. Investigate and report on how the structure and function of bones limit growth.

5. Investigate some of the limitations to human growth in the past. What limitations to growth do you think there will be in the next century?

Connection 4 Sampling in Nature and Industry

Sampling in Nature

To monitor the health of an animal species, wildlife officers keep records on the number of animals in a population. Because it is impossible to count each individual animal within a population, a sampling method known as the **capture-recapture method** is used to estimate the size of a wildlife population.

In order to estimate the deer population in a provincial park, wildlife officers randomly select and tag 50 deer. One year later they randomly select 250 deer and find that 4 deer had been tagged the year before. The officers can now estimate the total number of deer in the park using the following proportion.

$$\frac{n}{t} \doteq \frac{r}{s}$$

where n represents the original number of tagged animals
t represents the total number of animals
r represents the number of recaptured, tagged animals
s represents the number of animals in the second sample

In this example, we have

$$\frac{50}{t} \doteq \frac{4}{250}$$
$$4t \doteq 250 \times 50$$
$$4t \doteq 12\,500$$
$$t \doteq 3125$$

Thus, the officers estimate that there are approximately 3125 deer in the park.

Sampling in Industry

Canabyke Corporation has recently developed a new, safer trail bike. The job of Canabyke's marketing consultant is to conduct market research to determine what type of consumer would be interested in this product. The data collected from this research should indicate the attitudes of the market toward trail bikes. With this data Canabyke can choose the right marketing strategy to promote the trail bike.

Canabyke's marketing consultant feels that interest in the new trail bike is likely to vary with age, so the sample chosen is to be stratified by age. Since Canabyke plans to market the bike nationally, participants for the sample are chosen from several different communities in various provinces.

The analysis of data from the survey questionnaire shows that there is an interest in a safer trail bike. However, interest varies with age as this table illustrates.

Age of Respondents in Years	Percentage of Consumers Interested in New Trail Bike
16–25	48
26–35	24
36–45	17
over 45	8

As a result of its market research, Canabyke decides to use an advertising campaign that will stress the safety of the trail bike and will appeal to people between 16 and 25.

Explorations

1. Explain why the proportion used for estimating wildlife populations gives reasonable estimates.

2. Last year a group of wildlife officers in an arctic region captured and banded 150 arctic terns. This year the group captured 200 and found that 25 had already been banded. Estimate the number of arctic terns in the region.

3. If possible, invite a wildlife officer to speak to your class on the capturing-recapturing method. He or she might also discuss population

studies and their relationship to the granting of hunting and fishing licenses and the setting of seasons.

4. Suggest three questions that should be included in Canabyke's questionnaire.

5. Suppose you have invented a new computer game. How would you determine whether the game would appeal to a particular market?

6. Find out what cities in the U.S. are often chosen as test markets. Why do you think these particular cities are chosen? What kind of community would you choose as a test market and why?

7. Why do you think large companies conduct market research instead of putting their products directly on the market?

8. Suppose you are a manufacturer of some product that students would buy. Decide on a product, and determine whether there is a market for your product in your school or community.

Connection 5 Symmetry in Nature

Many organisms such as the ones shown seem to have reflection symmetry about a central plane. This means that a plane through their center seems to divide the organism into two parts that are mirror images of each other. Are these organisms really symmetrical?

If you were actually to compare the two halves of the organisms illustrated, you would see that they are not identical. For this reason these organisms are said to have *approximate* reflection symmetry.

Explorations

1. Using two mirrors, try to form a composite face with the left half of your face and its image. Comment on the differences between the composite and your own face. Repeat the procedure with the right side of your face and its image. Compare this composite with the first one.

2. Consult a biology textbook for more information on symmetry. Compare the definition of symmetry given in the biology text with one found in a mathematics text. Show examples of three types of symmetry found in organisms by using your own drawings or photographs if you like. Also show examples of organisms that are asymmetrical. Show how symmetry of an organism is related to its method of locomotion.

3. What role do you think symmetry plays in the perceived "beauty" of an organism?

Connection 6 Paleontology and Genealogy

It has long baffled scientists studying fossil records that so very many of the species that were alive in past ages have become extinct. Many theories have been put forward to explain this fact. Scientists have supposed that there must have been a series of cataclysmic events, disease, fires, earthquakes, great changes in climate, and so on.

A similar problem occurs in a very different field of learning, the study of family names. Historians studying English family names of the 14th century discovered that 75% of the names have died out and are not in current use. Since this is a period of relatively well-documented historic time, we know that no cataclysmic event occurred to wipe out whole extended families.

The resolution of these two similar questions has come about by creating a mathematical, computer-generated model of the situation.

In the evolutionary problem, the evolution of single species is modelled. Each time the species "breeds," there are three possibilities to which probabilities can be assigned: the species could continue in the same form; it could mutate to form a different species; the offspring could die. A family tree of such a species can be generated by a computer as shown in the graphic from the program *PALEOTREE*. As mutation occurs, other species are formed which either multiply or die out.

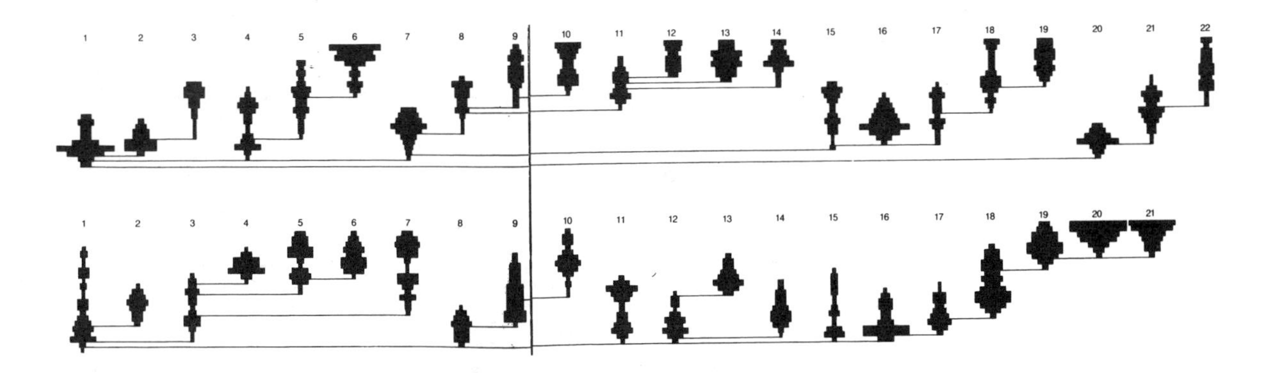

The "spindles" on the *PALEOTREE* diagram can be produced by hand by rolling a pair of dice to generate a tree. A sum of 2, 3, or 4 showing on the dice indicates that the species immediately dies out. If the sum is 9 or 10, the species diversifies and two short lines branch up from the dot. Any other sum indicates that the species does not change and a straight line is drawn upward from the dot. The number of dots at any given level can be plotted as the length of a bar in a spindle, as shown here.

A similar program can be written to trace surnames of successive generations of a family. Assuming that the family name is passed on through the male children (as has been the case in Western culture until recently), there are three possibilities. A couple could have male children,

A tree diagram showing speciation within a genus as determined by the roll of a pair of dice and the associated PALEOTREE spindle.

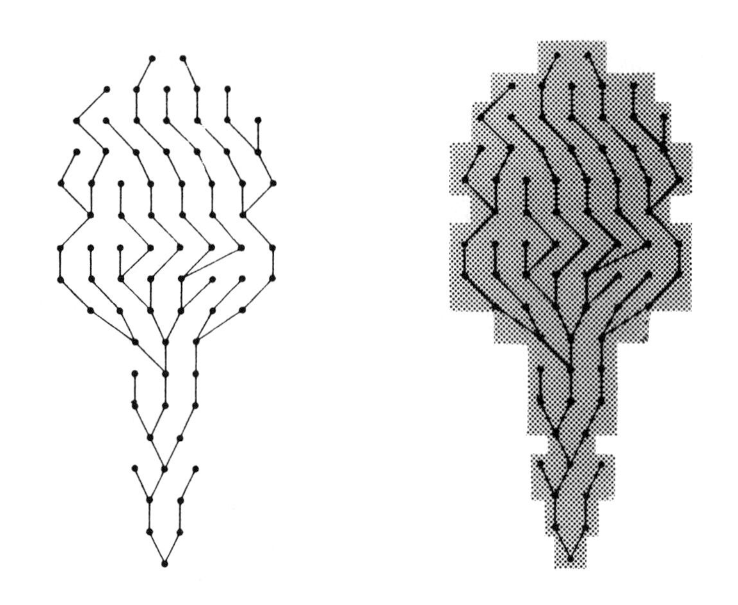

in which case the family name would be passed on; the couple could have female children, who marry and produce children with a different family name; the couple could have no surviving children. If these three possibilities are given suitable probabilities, the family trees which are then produced model (closely) those real-life cases which genealogists have documented.

The table below is used in a program which traces surnames. It is based on a statistical analysis of genealogical records. From the table, we see that the statistical probability that a family will produce no males who marry is 0.317. The assumption is that if the male marries, there is at least the *possibility* that the family name will be passed on.

Number of sons who marry	0	1	2	3	4	5	6
Probability	0.317	0.364	0.209	0.080	0.023	0.005	0.001

Results show that the extinction of about 75% of the species that were alive in the Paleozoic era is a natural consequence of the laws of probability. So is the disappearance of 75% of English family names of the 14th century.

Most mathematical models are great simplifications of the real world, with restrictions implied or explicit. Verification of models lies in comparing their predictions with data which scientists have already observed. When the results are very close to the observed data, it appears that the models are good.

Explorations

1. Investigate the genealogy of your extended family. If you have a fairly small number of relatives, start with the descendants of one

of your great-grandfathers. If your family is large, start with one of your grandfathers. How many males in your family will be likely to carry on the family name? (Assume that the pattern of passing on the name through male children only will continue.) Estimate the probability that the family name will continue for another hundred years.

2. Suppose a culture does not pass on the family name through male children only. Describe such a method and comment on how it affects the disappearance of family names.

3. Select a present-day species and investigate its family tree. When would you expect the species to become extinct under natural conditions?

4. Comment on humankind's role in the premature extinction of a particular species. Give an example of humankind's efforts to prevent the extinction of a species.

5. Find out more about the computer program *PALEOTREE* and report your findings. (See A. K. Dewdney, "Branching phylogenies of the Paleozoic and the fortunes of English family names," *Scientific American*, May 1986, pp. 16–22.)

Connection 7 The Human Body and Exponential Functions

Your body is constantly responding to a variety of stimuli, but you have no means of quantifying the *absolute* intensity of your sensations. You must judge their comparative values. It is only possible for you to observe that this object if heavier than that, or that one sound is louder than another.

There are experimental methods to determine an individual's judgment of the "just observable difference" between two stimuli to the same sense. Weber (1795–1878), a German physiologist, developed a way to investigate this "just observable difference."

In one series of experiments, the stimulus is increased by tiny increments until the subject just notices a change. In a second method, the subject must distinguish between two fairly close stimuli. A third method involves the subject's choosing a second stimulus equal to the first. In each case, you can infer that the individual has a subjective appreciation of the difference when that individual is able to state the difference correctly in just over 50% of the trails.

Weber discovered that the human body responds to a number of stimuli in a *logarithmic* fashion. That is, when you perceive a stimulus as increasing arithmetically, the stimulus is really increasing geometrically.

For example, if you can just distinguish a perceptible difference between 100 g and 80 g (20 g), then you will *not* be able to distinguish the

20 g difference between 160 g and 180 g. The best you will be able to just distinguish between is 160 g and 200 g because the *ratio* of the two masses, or the "*perception fraction*," remains constant.

$$\frac{80\text{ g}}{100\text{ g}} = \frac{160\text{ g}}{200\text{ g}}$$

As a consequence of the constant ratio requirement, the smallest (just) perceivable difference a person can appreciate varies with the intensity of the stimulus. Thus, if a person can only just distinguish that a 100 g object is heavier than an 80 g object, a 20 g difference, then that person could only just distinguish that a 125 g object is heavier than a 100 g object, a 25 g difference. In order to keep the ratio constant, the actual increase in mass must be greater in the second instance.

A generalization of the above example would read, "Noticeable differences in sensation occur when the increase in stimulus is a constant percentage of the stimulus itself." This generalization can be written symbolically as,

$$\frac{x_2 - x_1}{x_1} \times 100 = \frac{x_3 - x_2}{x_2} \times 100$$

or

$$\frac{x_2}{x_1} - 1 = \frac{x_3}{x_2} - 1$$

or

$$\frac{x_2}{x_1} = \frac{x_3}{x_2}$$

This implies that x_1, x_2, and x_3 are in geometric sequence, or in other words that x_1, x_2, and x_3 are the outputs of some exponential function. This is known as **Weber's law**. This law appears to hold for the sensations of touch (mass), sound, taste, smell, and visual brightness.

Explorations

1. Perform an experiment to see if you can distinguish between the mass of the following pairs and report the results.
   a. a pencil and a ruler
   b. a calculator and a note pad
   c. a sneaker and a calculator

2. Try to judge the temperature of bath water or a hot drink. Compare your guesses with actual temperature readings. Is your ability to judge cooler temperatures, such as the lake water you swim in, greater, less than, or about the same as your judgment of warmer temperatures?

3. Research some of the work Weber did. Try some of his experiments. Compare your "perception fractions" for touch, sound, taste, smell, or visual brightness with those of another class member.

4. Why do you think it is important to know that the human body responds to stimuli in a exponential fashion?

5. Interview an allergist or invite him or her to talk to your class about the “perception fractions” of people with allergies.

6. What do you think the relationship is between people’s “perception fractions” and the setting of pollution standards?

Biography

Connection 8

Ada Byron Lovelace—The First Computer Programmer

Today computers are used to perform not only mathematical calculations but also a wide variety of other tasks. In the early nineteenth century the principles of a computer system were developed by Charles Babbage in his plans for the Analytical Engine (a machine for performing calculations). It was Ada Byron Lovelace, a gifted mathematician, who helped Babbage develop the instructions for doing computations on the Analytical Engine. In developing these instructions, she was actually programming the Analytical Engine just as we program computers today. For this reason, Lovelace is recognized as the first computer programmer. A computer language sponsored by the Department of Defense in the United States has been dubbed ADA in her honor. Although Babbage did not build the Analytical Engine, Ada Lovelace published a series of notes that eventually led others to do so.

Explorations

1. Lady Lovelace was able to recognize the limitations of the Analytical Engine, stating that it could only do what it was told to do. How does this perception compare with today's argument that a computer by itself is not creative?
2. Do some research into the conditions and attitudes that were common in Lady Lovelace's time to determine why it was unusual for women to contribute to mathematics and science.
3. Read about and report on Babbage's Analytical Engine and Lady Lovelace's role in its eventual completion. What other contributions did Lady Lovelace make to mathematics?
4. Compare the design of Babbage's Analytical Engine to that of modern-day computers.

Connection 9

Eratosthenes (c. 276 B.C.–c. 194 B.C.)

Eratosthenes was a Greek mathematician. Very little is known about him since only a few fragments of his books remain, but he is recognized as one of the first to have accurately predicted the circumference of the earth.

Eratosthenes based his measurements on the assumption that the earth is round and the sun's rays are parallel. He knew that on the day of the summer solstice (June 21), a place on the Nile called Syene (now called Aswan) was directly beneath the sun. There were no shadows at noon and deep wells were illuminated by the sun's rays. At the same time in Alexandria, directly north of Syene, a vertical pole would cast a shadow. It was here that Eratosthenes performed a simple but effective experiment. He hammered a vertical pole into the ground and measured the height of the pole and the length of its shadow at noon on June 21.

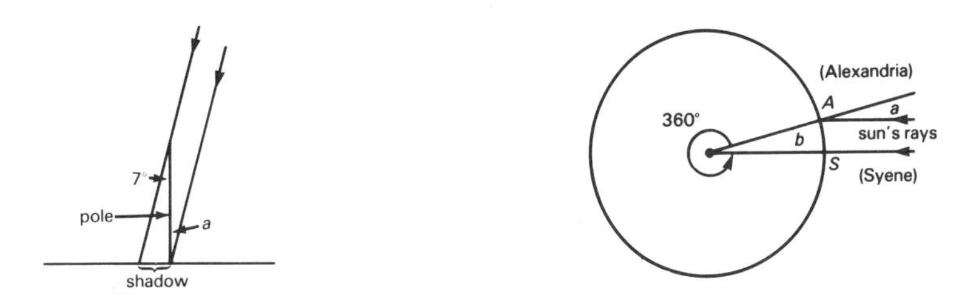

From his measurements Eratosthenes was able to calculate the angle between the pole and the sun's rays to be about 7°. He had found the value of a shown in the figures. Assuming that the sun's rays are parallel, he deduced that b was also about 7°. Can you explain why?

Since 7° is about one fiftieth of 360°, arc AS shown above is about one fiftieth of the earth's circumference. Eratosthenes concluded that the circumference of the earth must be about 50 times the distance between Alexandria and Syene. The circumference of the earth was found to be approximately 39 700 km.

Explorations

1. Find out more about the summer solstice. Would Eratosthenes's experiment have worked on any other day of the year? Explain why or why not.

2. Find out how the earth's circumference has been determined by other scientists since Eratosthenes's time. Compare the earth's circumference as found by Eratosthenes with today's accepted figure for it. What was Eratosthenes's percentage of error compared to today's accepted figure?

3. Explore other areas in mathematics for which Eratosthenes is known. Which of those areas interests you most? Explain why.

4. What do you think was Eratosthenes's most important contribution to mathematics? Explain your answer.

Connection 10

René Descartes

Graphs are used so widely today that they are no longer considered strictly mathematical devices. The slant of a line can give an immediate impression of how the sales of a product increase from year to year, the way the popularity of a government changes, or the way the height of a plant increases with time. Although the idea of graphing had occurred to several mathematicians, René Descartes was the first to develop the idea systematically.

Born in 1596 in Touraine, France, Descartes spent most of his adult life studying philosophy and mathematics. In 1637 he published *Discourse on the Method of Rightly Conducting the Reason* in which he described the technique of using a pair of numbers to determine a point on a surface. The pair of numbers, (x, y), are known as Cartesian coordinates, and the surface is known as the Cartesian plane. (The word Cartesian is derived from Cartesius, the Latin form of the name Descartes.)

Once Descartes was able to determine points on a plane, he could then express lines in terms of two points, and straight-line figures in terms of the points representing their vertices. Descartes extended this idea to draw equations as curves. By providing this important link between algebra and geometry, Descartes had developed a completely new way of looking at mathematical information.

Explorations

1. Descartes laid the foundation for other famous mathematicians who followed after him. Name two of these mathematicians and explain how each made use of Descartes's work.

2. Although Descartes is remembered primarily for his contribution to mathematics, his main interest was philosophy. Write a short essay discussing his philosophical ideas.

3. Graphs are often used to display data quickly and easily. What do you think are the characteristics of an effective graph? You might want to find examples of effective and ineffective graphs in magazines or newspapers. Suggest ways that the ineffective graphs could be improved.

4. Choose one or more of these curves to investigate.

witch of Agnesi	catenary	trochoid
cartioid	trisectrix	limaçon

Connection 11 Bertrand Russell

To describe Bertrand Russell is to list a series of contrasts. He was an aristocrat from a long–established family and also a staunch socialist; a mathematician responsible for many contributions towards the initial rigorous systematization of the logical foundations of mathematics and a novelist; a philosopher whose lectures to undergraduates were packed and who, during his time in America, had periodic discussions on metaphysics with a group that included Einstein; an almost fanatical leader of marches advocating nuclear disarmament, yet a pragmatist who realized the necessity for the West not to disarm totally after the end of World War II; the author of books on *Marriage and Morals* and *The Conquest of Happiness* who was three times divorced himself. All this, and much, much more, was accomplished in a lifetime begun in the Victorian Age on May 18, 1872, and lasting almost a full century until his death, on February 2, 1970. Russell was a man of indefatigable energy and concern for humanity who dictated an extremely controversial political statement concerning the situation in the Middle East only three days before his death.

A paradoxical man, he is also known for the Russell Paradox, which he discovered during his development of what is now called **set theory.** His major mathematical work was a book titled *Principia Mathematica,* which he wrote in collaboration with his former teacher at Cambridge University, Alfred North Whitehead (one of the few people from whom Russell would accept criticism willingly).

Mathematics was the major focus of Bertrand Russell's early life. When he was eleven years old, his elder brother introduced him to Euclidean geometry. "I had never imagined anything so delicious in the world," he said. Euclid pointed the young Russell on his road to philosophy.

The mathematical period of his life gradually led to his philosophical work, but in this early period (before World War I), his writings included *The Principles of Mathematics, An Essay on the Foundations of Geometry, Is Position in Time and Space Absolute or Relative?, Mathematical Logic* based on the *Theory of Types* (now called set theory), *The Study of Mathematics,* and *How to Become a Mathematician.*

The **Bertrand Russell Archives** were acquired by McMaster University in Hamilton, Ontario, Canada in 1968. The archives include a substantial part of Russell's correspondence. He wrote over 120 000 letters to prime ministers, presidents, heads of state, and acquaintances.

To find out more about this paradoxical man who was a distinguished mathematician as well as a winner of the Nobel Prize for literature (1950), you may want to read one of the many books written about him. Three such books are listed below.

The Life of Bertrand Russell, by R. W. Clark.
My Father, Bertrand Russell, by Katherine Tait.
Necessary Russell, by William Ready.

To Edith

Through the long years
I sought peace,
I found ecstasy, I found anguish,
I found madness,
I found loneliness.
I found the solitary pain
that gnaws the heart,
But peace I did not find.

Now, old & near my end,
I have known you,
And, knowing you,
I have found both ecstasy & peace,
I know rest,
After so many lonely years.
I know what life & love may be.
Now, if I sleep,
I shall sleep fulfilled.

Explorations

1. What is **The Russell Paradox?** What is its significance?

2. Here is an example of the kind of paradox Russell discovered. Consider the statement "All generalizations are false." The statement itself is a generalization. It can't be true because all generalizations are false. But if it's false, the statement would have to say that generalizations are true. So it can't be true and it can't be false. Write your own example of a paradox.

3. Find out more about Bertrand Russell's political activism. How were Einstein's political views similar to Russell's? In what ways do you think their political views influenced their professional work? Give examples to support your answer.

4. Both Descartes and Russell had interests in philosophy. How do you think that mathematics and philosophy are related?

5. Read from one of Russell's books or essays. What did you find most interesting in the reading? Did your reading help you to understand Russell or his work better? Explain.

Connection 12 H. S. M. Coxeter

In 1985, a book was published in the United States by Birkhauser–Boston called *Mathematical People.* This book, edited by Donald Albers and Gerald Alexanderson, contains in-depth interviews with twenty-four prominent and influential people in mathematics. Among these twenty-four mathematicians is H. S. M. Coxeter. Coxeter, who has been teaching at the University of Toronto since 1936, is considered to be one of the most important geometricians living today.

Mathematics as a science is divided into many subsections. In high school, you obtain only a meager glimpse of the mathematics that has been discovered or invented. You are familiar with those parts of mathematics that you know as geometry, algebra, trigonometry, vectors, probability, calculus, and combinatorics. Mathematicians are continually discovering new ideas concerned with each of these branches of mathematics. In addition, they invent new kinds of mathematics.

University mathematicians such as Coxeter have a two-fold task. One is to teach mathematics to students; the other is to do research in their particular field, that is, to discover new ideas. Coxeter has been a world leader in both respects for many years.

As a teacher, Coxeter has the uncanny ability to make difficult ideas so clear that they appear simple. One of his students recalls a lecture by a certain professor where that professor spent an hour proving some abstract mathematical theorem. A few days later the student attended a lecture by Coxeter, who proved the same theorem by a much more understandable method. Coxeter's proof took less than ten minutes!

Coxeter is a world leader in geometry research. He has authored or co-authored over 140 articles published in mathematics journals. Each of these articles has added new ideas to the knowledge of geometry. In addition, Coxeter has written eleven books on various aspects of geometry. His unorthodox view of the world in general, education, and mathematics can be appreciated by reading the interview he gave for the book *Mathematical People.* The following excerpts from that interview will give you some insights into Coxeter, the man and mathematician.

> *(at sixteen) I was already doing things on polytopes which later became the climax of chapter 11 of my book,* Regular Polytopes; *but all the standard stuff in algebra, geometry, analysis, and even applied mathematics, which I would have to do, I knew scarcely anything about.*
>
> *Geometry, I suppose, is the study of shapes and patterns.*
>
> *I think English-speaking people seem to have abandoned geometry because there was a tradition of dull teaching, perhaps too much emphasis on axiomatics went on for a long time.*
>
> *Geometry is developing as fast as any other kind of mathematics. It's just that people are not looking at it.*

Until he was 16, Coxeter was considering a career as a musician. When asked why he changed directions, he replied, "My mother took me to visit some musicians. They looked at my stuff and were not too impressed." Still, later in his life, Coxeter did publish an article on "Music and Mathematics."

A geometer, a theorist, a musician, a teacher, a writer, a scholar, a mathematician, Coxeter demonstrates what seems to be the common link among all great thinkers—an enormous involvement with life.

Explorations

1. Coxeter mentions in his interview that the topics he would include in a "nice" geometry curriculum would be inversive and projective geometry. Find out what these two geometries involve and give examples from each area.

2. Do some research to find out about some of the newest fields of mathematics. What do you think is the significance or importance of the new work being done? Prepare a list of names of the leaders exploring the new fields including the names of the countries and organizations they represent as well as the area of mathematics each is studying. Comment on any patterns you might see.

3. Select one person that you found for the previous question and prepare a display that will explain some aspect of the mathematician's work and any personal information about the mathematician that you feel is interesting.

4. It has been said that mathematicians tend to make their contributions of new knowledge at a relatively early age. Coxeter mentions doing original work on polytopes at age sixteen, for example. How do the ages at which scientists or artists (including musicians, painters, and writers) make their contributions to new knowledge compare to the ages when mathematicians make their contributions? If mathematicians do, in fact, "ripen" early, why do you think this is so?

Connection 13 Sonya Kovalevskaya

Sonya Kovalevskaya (1850–1891) was the second child of an aristocratic Russian family. Her love of mathematics was inspired by her favorite uncle, Peter, when she was very young. Later, she spent hours trying to decipher some old calculus notes that she found at home. This first attempt helped her greatly when she studied calculus formally at the age of 15 in St. Petersburg. At that time there were many obstacles facing women who wanted to study. Russian universities were closed to women and single women were not supposed to travel abroad alone. So Kovalevskaya contracted a marriage of convenience to a promising young writer, Vladimir Kovalevsky. In 1869, they travelled to Heidelburg, the oldest and most respected university in Germany. Here, as well as studying mathematics, she heard Kirchhoff and Helmholtz lecture in physics and met the chemist Bunsen. In 1870, she travelled to Berlin to study with the great mathematician Weierstrass, in spite of the fact that Berlin University was also closed to women. In the four years that she was in Berlin, she completed the university course in mathematics and wrote several important papers. Her doctoral thesis concerned partial differential equations. In 1874, Kovalevskaya was granted her doctorate by the University of Göttingen.

In 1883, Kovalevskaya went to Stockholm, where the climate was more favorable for women in academic life. She was appointed to the position of university professor and continued to produce a wide variety of mathematical papers. The high point of her career came in 1888, when she was awarded the Prix Bordin of the French Academy of Sciences. In the following year, the Stockholm Academy of Sciences also awarded her a prize. In 1889, she became the first female member of the Russian Academy of Sciences.

Throughout her life, Kovalevskaya managed to combine her interest in mathematics with a keen interest in literature. As a teenager, she had an article published in a magazine edited by Dostoevsky. Later in her life, she wrote: "All my life I have been unable to decide for which I had the greater inclination, mathematics or literature. As soon as my brain grows weary of purely abstract speculations, it immediately begins to incline to observations on life, to narrative, and vice versa, everything in life begins to appear insignificant and uninteresting, and only the eternal immutable laws of science attract me."

Explorations

1. The following quote is from Sonya Kovalevskaya, her *Recollections of Childhood* translated by Isabel Hapgood (New York: The Century Co., 1895, p. 316).

   It seems to me that the poet has only to perceive that which others do not perceive, to look deeper than others look. And the mathematician must do the same thing.

What do you think she meant by this statement? Explain why you agree or disagree.

2. Find out what types of problems were of interest to mathematicians during Kovalevskaya's time. What do you think was the importance of her work to mathematics and science?

3. In what ways do you think mathematics and literature are related?

Connection 14 Emmy Noether

Emmy Noether (1882–1935) was the daughter of a university professor and mathematician. She grew up in Erlangen, Germany, at a time when higher education was becoming more accessible for women. However, when she entered Erlangen University in 1900, she was one of only two women among one thousand students enrolled. She completed her doctoral thesis in 1907. Also, she sometimes substituted as a lecturer for her father. In 1916, she went to the University of Göttingen where she became a respected colleague of the great mathematicians Felix Klein and David Hilbert. Prejudice against women prevented her from becoming a full professor until she came to the United States in 1933. Hermann Weyl wrote of the injustice of the situation: "From 1930–33, she was the strongest centre of mathematical activity there [in Göttingen], considering both the fertility of her scientific research program and her influence upon a large circle of pupils." When she read a summary of her work at the International Congress in Zurich in 1932, she was finally given the recognition that she so richly deserved.

In 1933, Noether left Germany, together with many other Jewish scholars and intellectuals, as the power of the Nazi party increased in that country. She became a professor at Bryn Mawr and lectured at the Institute for Advanced Study at Princeton. Noether's work was mainly in the field of abstract algebra. If you continue your studies in mathematics you will soon meet the ideas in this field.

At the time of Noether's death, Einstein wrote in the *New York Times*: "In the judgment of the most competent living mathematicians, Fräulein Noether was the most significant creative mathematical genius thus far produced since the higher education of women began."

Explorations

1. Hermann Weyl wrote that Emmy Noether "changed the face of algebra by her work." (Hermann Weyl, "Emmy Noether," *Scripta Mathematica,* VIII, 3 (July 1935), p. 207.) Read more about her work to find out why he made this statement.

2. In what ways do you think Emmy Noether's and Sonya Kovalevskaya's experiences as women mathematicians were similar? How were they different?

3. Suppose you are a mathematical historian. Write a short biography of a present-day female mathematician. Include some information about the areas of mathematics that interest her. You may also want to comment on how her experiences with discrimination compare with those of Noether and Kovalevskaya.

Business

Connection 15

Probability in Insurance

Life is full of risks. People try to protect themselves and their families from the financial loss associated with risk through purchase of insurance. Insurance coverage for financial loss from accident, death, fire, or loss of a job is common. These types of insurance may provide payment when a wage earner is unable to work, payment for medical expenses resulting from illness or accident, payment for loss of a house due to fire, or damages arising from an automobile accident.

Insurance companies provide many types of protection. Individuals who want to be insured against particular kinds of losses make regular payments for insurance protection. In return, the companies agree to pay certain sums to the individuals if the particular losses involved occur. All people buying insurance share the costs of these payments for losses through their regular payments, called premiums. Even if purchasers never suffer a loss and therefore do not receive any money from the insurance company, they will have been afforded a feeling of security.

In order for insurance companies to make a profit, after paying clients for losses and meeting administrative costs, they must be able to predict the likelihood that an insured person will suffer a loss. **Probability** plays an important role in making this prediction.

The information shown in Table 1 was collected to determine premium rates for automobile insurance. This information can be used to find answers to questions about the probability that a certain individual will have a claim and the average cost of the reimbursement involved. Note that the table groups individuals by age, sex, and marital status. These categories have traditionally been used by companies in establishing rates.

Life insurance companies must be able to predict how long a person might live before deciding whether or not to issue insurance and what premium should be charged if the person qualifies for the insurance. Certain health conditions or types of life style may make a person ineligible for life insurance. Mortality tables like Table 2 are used to calculate the probability that a person will live to a particular age. This table is based on statistics gathered from U.S., British, and Canadian insurance company records. Historically, mortality rates are figured separately for males and females. The data here begin with 1,000,000 male births.

Table 1

Group	Number of Claims per 100 Cars	Average Claim Cost (Property and Bodily Injury)
Males (unmarried)		
18 and under	22.49	$3249
19–20	15.47	$3533
21–22	11.61	$3625
23–24	9.52	$3454
Males (married)		
20 and under	14.97	$4035
21–24	8.80	$3009
Females		
20 and under	7.19	$2714
21–24	5.46	$2737
Male or Female 25 and under	6.51	$2998

Table 2

Age Group (years)	Number Living through 10-year period	Deaths in 10-year period	Deaths per 1000 people
0–9	992014	7986	7.99
10–19	986761	5253	5.25
20–29	976596	10165	10.17
30–39	965472	11124	11.12
40–49	936750	28722	28.72
50–59	860201	76549	76.55
60–69	676273	183928	183.93
70–79	376636	299637	299.64
80–89	92516	284120	284.12
90–99	4120	88396	88.40
100–110	0	4120	4.12

Explorations

1. How do you think claims statistics like those shown in Table 1 affect insurance rates for male versus female drivers, married versus unmarried drivers, and teen versus middle-aged drivers? Do you think the use of data such as these for establishing premium rates is appropriate? Why?

2. Use Table 2 to look at death rates in the first 10 years of life as compared to the second 10 years. What might account for the difference?

3. Invite a panel of insurance agents to speak to your class about life or automobile insurance options. Analyze the various options and the premiums charged for each. Which options would you choose and why?

Connection 16 Linear Programming

A small manufacturing company produces high-quality professional hockey skates. Two models are produced by the company: the Excalibur (at a profit of $40 per pair) and the Faultless (at a profit of $30 per pair). The company's manufacturing plant can produce up to 60 pairs of the Excalibur or up to 90 pairs of the Faultless per week, but no more than 120 pairs in total per week. How many pairs of each model should be produced each week to maximize profit?

Solution

Let x represent the number of pairs of the Excalibur produced per week. Let y represent the number of pairs of the Faultless produced per week. Let P represent the weekly profit in dollars.

$0 \leqslant x \leqslant 60$ ← **Since** the number of skates cannot be negative, values for x and y must be positive.

$0 \leqslant y \leqslant 90$ ←

$x + y \leqslant 120$

$P = 40x + 30y$

Graph the region that is common to the three inequalities listed above. (Why must you use points instead of lines for this graph?) It can be shown that maximum (or minimum) values occur at corners or vertices of a region. Substitute the x and y values at each vertex into the profit equation to determine which pair of values will produce the maximum profit.

Vertex (x, y)	Profit ($) $P = 40x + 30y$
(0, 90)	2700
(30, 90)	3900
(60, 60)	4200
(60, 0)	2400

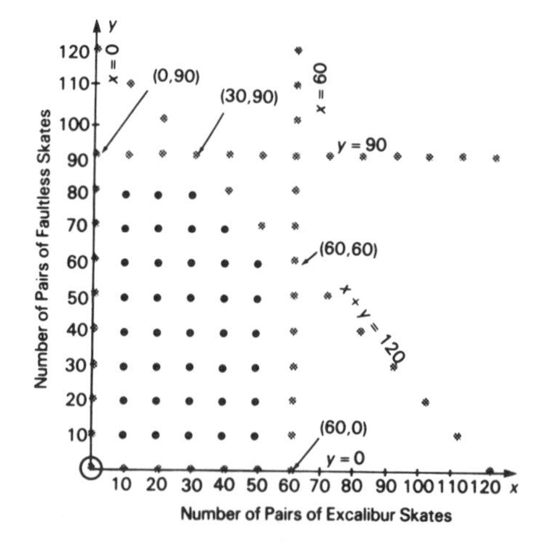

The maximum profit of $4200 occurs when 60 pairs of each type of skate are produced.

The example above was solved using techniques of **linear programming.** Linear programming involves finding a minimum or maximum solution of a problem that can be expressed using only linear equations and inequalities.

The skate manufacturing company wanted to maximize profit, which they were able to express as a linear equation $P = 40x + 30y$. Additionally, the process was subject to several linear constraints:

They could produce at most 60 pairs of Excalibur or 90 pairs of Faultless models, but no more than 120 pairs in total. These constraints were expressed in the three linear inequalities given in the example.

We knew from the mathematical theory of linear programming that the maximum values required to solve this problem occur at the vertices of the region defined by the equations and inequalities in the original expression and given constraints.

Explorations

1. Mario Donnetti runs the Sound Emporium, where he sells cassettes and records. To provide customers with an adequate selection of titles, he feels he must maintain a total inventory of at least 3500 cassettes and records. Mario also feels that he should stock no fewer than 1000 cassettes and 1500 records. His inventory costs for cassettes and records are \$5 and \$8 respectively. How many cassettes and records should he stock to minimize his inventory costs? What is the minimum inventory cost? Use x to represent the number of cassettes and y to represent the number of records. Use the following information.

$$x + y \geqslant 3500$$

$$x \geqslant 1000$$

$$y \geqslant 1500$$

Inventory costs C (dollars) can be represented by the equation $C = 5x + 8y$.

2. Three graphs are shown below. Choose one and do the following problems associated with it.
   a. Write a linear equation or inequality to describe each of the boundary lines of the region shown on the graph.
   b. Let the expression below the graph represent the quantity you want to either maximize or minimize. Describe a problem that meets the conditions of the given constraints and can be represented by the given expression. For example, you may want to let the expression equal cost rather than profit. Then it would be logical to find the minimum value of the equation.
   c. Exchange problems with a friend and solve each other's problems.

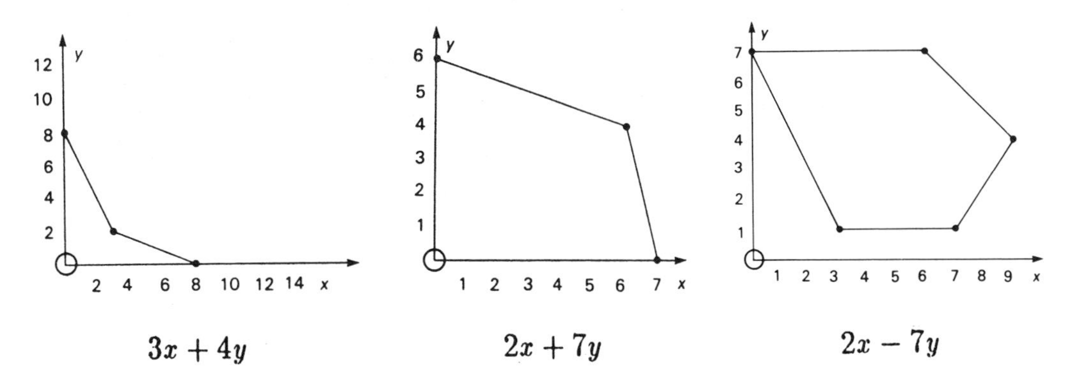

$3x + 4y$ $2x + 7y$ $2x - 7y$

3. Do some research into the history of linear programming to find out how and why it was developed. Explain how it is used in decision-making for large-scale industrial processes.

Connection 17 May I Have Your Opinion?

Mathematics has a great impact on our lives through the use of statistics in opinion polls.

Politicians use the results of the polls to help themselves understand what is wanted and valued by their constituents.

Market researchers use surveys to determine which products will sell successfully, and to whom.

Network television programs are cancelled or renewed on the basis of their Nielson ratings, the product of surveys.

The outcomes of elections are predicted with some accuracy, well before the first vote is cast.

The mathematical basis for using surveys in the situations above is **statistical inference**. A pollster uses the methods of statistical inference to infer the opinions of a large population from those of a relatively small sample. In addition to predicting the opinions of a large group from a smaller subgroup's opinions, the pollster can also use statistical techniques to determine the probability that the predictions are correct.

Informal opinion polls have been around for a long time. Early surveys about which candidate was favored in a political election were known as **straw polls**.

The modern history of opinion polls begins in 1935. In the early twentieth century, *The Literary Digest* would send out, before each presidential election, as many as 18 million cards to its readers, soliciting the readers' preference of candidate. As many as 2 million readers responded. On the basis of this sampling, the *Digest* was able to accurately predict the outcome of each presidential election (of 1932 and earlier). *The Literary Digest* ran its poll again in 1936 when the Republican, Alf Landon, ran against the Democrat candidate, Franklin D. Roosevelt. The prediction, based on the poll results, was that Landon would win the election.

In 1935, a group of statisticians and pollsters, George Gallup, Roger Crossley, and Elmo Archibald, formed the American Institute of Public Opinion. The Institute favored a more scientific approach to sampling data and interpreting the results. Using a far smaller sample of opinions than *The Literary Digest*, the Institute was able to accurately predict that Roosevelt would defeat Landon in the election.

One result of this success by the Institute was that *The Literary Digest* soon ceased publication. Another result was that the methods promoted by Gallup and his colleagues became so pervasive in society that the term Gallup poll became very well known.

Here are some of the problems a pollster must address.

How large (or small) a sample will allow an accurate prediction?

How do you ensure a true opinion from the person being surveyed?

How do you ensure that the sample is unbiased, that is, truly representative of the population about which you are drawing inferences?

Explorations

1. Using newspapers or magazines, find an example of an opinion poll. How much faith do you have in the results of the poll? Why? How would you have answered the questions asked in the poll? Conduct a survey using the same questions. Suggest explanations for any significant differences you find. In structuring your survey, remember to address the questions pollsters must consider.

2. Look through recent copies of your local newspaper to find an issue that caused controversy in your town. Conduct a survey in your school or neighborhood to measure opinions on the issue in question. Report your findings. Use graphs or charts wherever possible to present your data.

Computers

Connection 18 Revolutions

There are many different kinds of revolutions that can cause changes in society. Often a revolution results in a complete, and sometimes violent, overthrow of an established government or political system. The French Revolution, the Russian Revolution, and the Hungarian Revolution are examples of this type of revolution. Not all revolutions, however, are political. They may also occur in cultural, social, and industrial areas. In the 1700s and early 1800s, for example, the Industrial Revolution transformed the Western world from a rural society to an urban and industrial society.

Today we find ourselves in the middle of an **information revolution** which will result in dramatic changes in the way we live, perhaps even in the way we think. At the heart of this revolution is, of course, the computer. Computers are used in almost every conceivable area: from graphics to medicine and robotics; from commerce and transportation to education and entertainment.

Explorations

1. Why do you think that the growth in information has been termed a revolution? Investigate and report on this phenomenon. Use graphing techniques you have learned to present data about the amount of information available now versus thirty years ago. See if you can also express this information growth algebraically as a function of time.

2. What is the rate of growth in information over the last thirty years? Is that rate the same as the one expressed by your function and the slope of your graph?

3. How do you think computers have affected the information revolution? Compare the amount of storage in a small personal computer

to that in a thirty-year-old computer. Compare the speed of processing data in a small personal computer to that of a thirty-year-old computer.

4. Try to find out the cost of a computer thirty years ago and compare it with the cost of a small personal computer today.

5. Keep a journal of the ways in which your life is directly affected by computers over a one-week period. Compare your journal with those of your classmates. In what ways do you think these computer influences have improved the quality of your life? Are there ways in which computers have had a negative impact on your life?

Connection 19 Flight Simulation

Many of you will have learned to drive recently. First of all, you probably took a test on the rules of the road and had your eyesight checked. Then, assuming you passed those tests, you started to drive a real car on a public road with a licensed driver beside you.

This process works quite well when you are learning to drive a car. However, learning to fly is a very different proposition. In the case of a large passenger jet plane, the lives of over five hundred passengers and millions of dollars worth of equipment are at stake. Any pilot has to learn not only how to fly under normal conditions, but also how to deal with severe weather, engine failure, and perhaps even hostage-taking incidents. A pilot cannot stop a plane in the middle of a flight to read the manual or ask for directions.

Most pilots of commercial and military aircrafts are trained in a flight simulator. A flight simulator consists of the cockpit of an aircraft in which all the controls and instruments are connected to a computer. A separate control room monitors and records a pilot's lessons. For example, if a pilot increases the throttle, the signal from the throttle is transmitted to the computer. Using a series of mathematical equations, the computer changes the readings on the instruments to simulate changes in speed, altitude, and fuel level resulting from the increase in the throttle. The computer can also be programmed so that the instruments indicate to the trainee pilot that an engine has failed, that fuel is being lost, or that there is a fire in some location in the plane. The pilot's response to these emergencies can then be evaluated. If the pilot fails to land safely the first time, he or she can have a second or third try at dealing with the same emergency.

In addition to being able to read the instruments in a real cockpit, a trained pilot can use the view from the cockpit to help in flying the plane. This is particularly useful during landing and takeoff, the most critical times on any flight. In a simulator, a screen replaces the cockpit window. The image on the screen displays the view that a pilot would have at each instant of a flight. The computer calculates the position of the plane at any particular moment from its speed and direction, and produces the images on the screen.

Statistics on wartime pilots indicate that most pilots who are killed are killed within their first five flights. If a pilot survives the first five flights, his or her probability of surviving additional flights rises 95% . If the first five flights for trainee pilots can be simulated, much loss of life can be eliminated.

Flight simulators can also be used to evaluate different training programs and to carry out fundamental research on visual perception. Flight simulation has also become a very popular computer game. Various keys on the computer keyboard represent the throttle, the ailerons, the rudder, and other controls. The screen displays the scenery and a simplified version of the instrument panel. In some of the games, the geographic data are very realistic. The mathematical problems of creating a changing image of a three-dimensional object as seen from a moving aircraft are very challenging. These problems are the same for programmers of flight simulators and programmers of computer games.

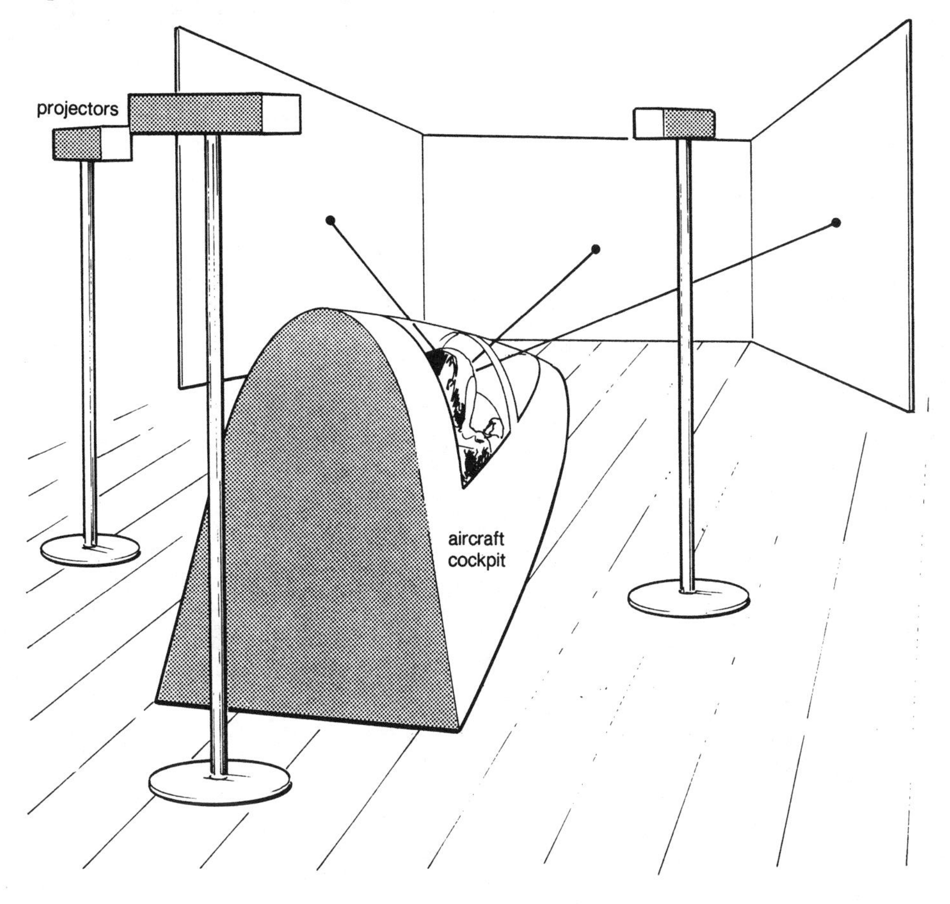

Explorations

1. Find some examples other than flight simulation where computer simulation is particularly valuable. What are the benefits of these simulations corresponding with the improved safety and reduced expense involved in training pilots through flight simulation?

2. Do you think that computer simulation programs should be developed for beginning automobile drivers? Why or why not?

3. You have learned the basic formula expressing distance as a function of rate and time, $d = r \times t$. A simulation device for driving a vehicle must express motion as a function of many variables; for example, the shape of the vehicle may affect the speed and acceleration. (A truck responds differently from a car when turning corners or driving in a wind or rain storm.) See if you can find other factors which must be taken into account when developing a driving simulator. What mathematical techniques that you have learned might be useful in this simulator? Do you think that there will be many equations or

only one? Do you think that the relationships will be linear? Can you think of ways in which inequalities might be involved? Which of the factors that you identified as important for a driving simulator would also be important for a flight simulator? Which situation do you think is more complex? Why?

Connection 20 Secret Codes and Large Primes

Most people accept the fact that governments need secret codes to transmit important secret information around the world. But it is only recently, with the advent of high-speed computers, that businesses have seen the need for such codes.

The science of cryptography uses various methods for writing in secret code or cipher. As society becomes increasingly dependent upon computers, the vast amounts of data communicated, processed, and stored within our computer systems and computer networks often have to be protected. Cryptography is a practical method for protecting such information which is frequently transmitted through communication networks such as telephone lines, satellites, or microwave systems. Access to the information that is transmitted in these ways is easy to attain. If the information is not coded, then anyone can use it.

In the most basic type of cipher or secret code, each letter of the alphabet is assigned a different number. For example: 1–A, 2–B, 3–C, . . . , 25–Y, 26–Z. Thus the message "I love math" would be encoded as "9, 12, 15, 22, 5, 13, 1, 20, 8." Because this basic code is easy to decode or break, people have continually searched for more difficult codes. Julius Caesar used a code in which each letter of the alphabet was replaced by the third letter following it in the cyclic order of the alphabet. Thus, the message "I love math" would become "LORYHPDWK." Such a code is more difficult to break than the basic code but decoding it is still relatively easy.

A **public key cryptography system** is a code in which the information used for coding need not be secret. Thus, anyone in possession of the encoding key, which is two numbers h and n, can send a message, but only those in possession of a further decoding key number d can read the message. For example, the public key described in a lecture given by the Faculty of Science at Simon Fraser University in British Columbia is a modern code that depends for its security on the difficulty of factoring, into prime factors, very large numbers that have one hundred or more digits.

Example

Assume you wish to encode the single word message "ME." Since M and E are the 13th and 5th letters of the alphabet, respectively, represent "ME" by the number 135.

Further, suppose you have selected $h = 7$ and $n = 187$ as your public key numbers.

Then, the message in code is the number c which equals the remainder after 135^h has been divided by n. Using a computer to divide 135^7 by 187, you would obtain a remainder of 152. Thus your encoded message is $c = 152$.

The person who received this message needs the secret key number d to decode the message. As will be explained later, $d = 23$. To obtain the decoded message, a computer would be used to divide $c^d = 152^{23}$ by $n = 187$. The remainder will be the original number 135.

If you wish to send the message "MATH", you would encode the number 131208 in the same manner.

But how are public key and secret key numbers selected? To obtain the public key number n, two very large prime numbers p and q, each over 50 digits in length, are used. These numbers are kept secret, but their product $pq = n$ is made public.

The secret primes p and q determine the public key h and the secret key d. h and d can be any numbers such that their product hd has a remainder of 1 after division by $(p-1)(q-1)$. For someone to find the secret key d, the person would need to know both p and q. Even though $n = pq$ is readily obtained, centuries of high–speed computer calculation could be necessary to find the prime factors p and q. It is this difficulty of determining p and q that has made public key cryptography codes almost impossible to break.

Continuing, we apply this procedure to the example above, where $n = 187$. Expressing 187 as 11×17, then $p = 11$ and $q = 17$. h and d are chosen so that hd has a remainder of 1 after division by $(p-1)(q-1) = 10 \times 16 = 160$. $hd = 161$ is such a number. Since $161 = 7 \times 23$, one number, say 7, is selected as h and the other, 23, as d.

Explorations

1. Encode a short message of your own using $n = 10$ and $h = 11$ as the public key numbers and $d = 3$ as the secret code. Now encode another short message selecting a different n and h. (For simplicity, keep p and q small.) See if someone else can break your code by finding d.

2. The first hundred primes appear in the table below. Can a prime number ever end in the digit 5? 8? 3? The prime number 13 can be written as $4 \cdot 3 + 1$. Can you find three other primes that can be written in the form $4n + 1$?

   Think of some other questions about primes. Exchange questions with one of your classmates.

The First Hundred Prime Numbers														
2	3	5	7	11	13	17	19	23	29	31	37	41	43	47
53	59	61	67	71	73	79	83	89	97	101	103	107	109	113
127	131	137	139	149	151	157	163	167	173	179	181	191	193	197
199	211	223	227	229	233	239	241	251	257	263	269	271	277	281
283	293	307	311	313	317	331	337	347	349	353	359	367	373	379
383	389	397	401	409	419	421	431	433	439	443	449	457	461	463
467	479	487	491	499	503	509	521	523	541					

3. Read more about cryptography systems. Describe one or two that you find interesting. Include comments about difficulties with the system. Do you think an unbreakable code can be invented? Why or why not? Find examples from history when code-breaking has played a significant role in international politics.

4. Ask a local business person (perhaps a banker) to discuss the role of cryptography in protecting business information.

Connection 21 Information, Please

One name that has been used to describe the latter part of the twentieth century is the Age of Information. You live in a world which has a telephone network involving over half a billion telephones. Radio signals from space probes come to earth and are converted into breath-taking photographs of the planets. Television, radio, newspapers, magazines, and books disseminate staggering quantities of the abstraction known as information.

Modern society depends on the rapid and accurate transmission of huge volumes of information. Many of the technological advances which help the world to cope with information flow have as their theoretical underpinning a branch of probability theory known as **information theory**.

Information theory is concerned with the likelihood of the transmission of messages. The theory is concerned with how much of a message will be received when one looks at the probabilities of transmission failure, distortion, and accidental additions of information called "noise." Information theory also shows the theoretical maximum amount of information that can be transmitted in a given situation. This is useful for communication engineers who wish to know just how much information can be transmitted if the information is properly coded and packed before transmission.

The components of an information transmission are sketched in the diagram below.

information source *message* *input*	⟶	transmitter *signal*	⟶ ↑ NOISE	receiver *received signal*	⟶	destination *message* *output*

There is no such thing as perfect transmission of information. Information is lost, distorted, or added in the transmission process. The goal of communication is to ensure that the receiver has enough information in the output message to determine the contents of the input message within specified limits of accuracy.

Communication engineers armed with the probabilities of loss, distortion, and noise can work to optimize the transmission of information. That is, for a given transmission channel, what is the greatest transmission rate of information which will permit the reception of messages with an acceptable level of error?

Information theory began with the work of one remarkable person, Claude Shannon. He is an American engineer/applied mathematician who has done research for the Bell Telephone Laboratories and other important work in the fields of computing machines, cryptography, and communications. It was Shannon, in papers written in 1938 and 1949, who demonstrated how Boolean algebra could be applied to switching circuits and hence, computers. It was also Shannon who coined the term "bit" for binary digit which is so common in computer jargon today.

Shannon's most significant contribution, however, may have been his invention of information theory. He first presented his theory in the 1948 research paper *The Mathematical Theory of Communication.*

Information theory has changed the manner in which we regard information. Prior to Shannon's paper, many were aware of the problems being caused by the increasing flow of information over the available transmission channels, but information was a vague, unquantified concept which defied engineering analysis. Shannon showed how to deal with information in much the same way a physicist might deal with thermal engineering. His work paved the way for many rapid and significant advances in telecommunications.

The equation used to identify the average amount of information which can be transmitted in a given situation is a sum of probabilities. The equation is identical in form to an equation describing the motion of particles due to random collisions. The probability theory in information theory is identical to that used in statistical mechanics to predict the most likely behavior of individual atoms and molecules.

Another interesting concept in information theory is redundancy. Because of the nature of the message being transmitted, it is sometimes possible to recode the message so that the recoded message is more compact than the original message and so that there is still a high probability that the message can be understood. For example, because of the statistical frequency of letters in English, the average information per letter in an English message is about 1 bit. Information theory states that English is about 80% redundant. A message in English can be efficiently recoded, transmitted, and accurately decoded using far fewer characters than the original.

N THR WRDS, NGLSH CN B WRTTN MR
CMPCTLY ND STLL B NDRSTD!

Explorations

1. Compare the shortened version of the English message example to its original form. What is the percentage of redundancy in the original as compared to the example given here?

2. a. Substitute two different letters in two different places in the abbreviated sample to represent transmission errors. Is it still possible to understand the message?
   b. Substitute different letters for three consecutive characters in the abbreviated message and see if it is still possible to understand the message.
   c. Which of these two types of transmission errors do you think is more serious?

3. Do you remember playing a party game called "Telephone" as a child? In that game one person starts a message and each person around the

table whispers the message he or she hears to the next person. What usually happens in that game? Relate the game to the diagram of the components of information transmission. Describe each of the terms in the diagram as they occur in the game.

4. Information transmission is one element of the process of education. Describe one way in which information theory can be applied to help solve a problem relating to education.

Connection 22 Game Theory

John von Neumann

Few mathematical theories developed in the twentieth century have generated as much interest or caused as much controversy as the theory of games. The theory of games draws heavily from probability theory and matrix theory, but it is a distinct mathematical field of itself.

Some of the seminal ideas of game theory were introduced in the 1920s. The theory itself was first completely presented in the massive work *Theory of Games and Economic Behavior* in 1944. The authors were John von Neumann and Oskar Morgenstern. Morgenstern was an economist and von Neumann was one of the most brilliant mathematicians of the twentieth century.

The theory of games is a mathematical analysis of situations involving the rational behavior of two or more people whose interests are in conflict. The theory is sometimes thought of as the applied mathematics of economic and social behavior.

Originally the theory had as many critics as proponents. Economists and social scientists felt that the theory tried to deal with phenomena that were too varied and complex for a single theory. But ironically, even in criticizing the theory, these scientists began to use the language and concepts of the theory of games.

The language of the theory of games is evocative. Without developing the theory here, we can still look at some of concepts.

A **strategy** is a behavior that one or more of the persons can adopt.

A **two-person, zero-sum** game is a situation where the winnings of one person exactly equal the losses of the other. Von Neumann proved the famous minimax theorem for such games. The minimax theorem states that for each player a strategy exists that minimizes the maximum loss the other player can impose on the first. The study of non-zero-sum games are of importance in situations such as labor disputes where labor and management can choose behaviors which allow both sides to "win."

Mixed strategies occur when a player chooses actions at random from a set of options.

The **Shapley-Shubik power index** gives a measure of a stockholder's voting influence when the number of shares held in a company is the only consideration.

Does anyone take game theory seriously in practical considerations? The yacht *Stars and Stripes*, winner of the America's Cup sailing competition in 1987, was designed partially using the results of game theory.

Explorations

1. Make two lists, one of zero-sum games and one of non-zero-sum games. To do this, you should think broadly of a game as a situation

in which there are at least two parties who may be in competition, or think that they are. Is chess a zero-sum game? Is marriage? Discuss your reasons for placing each situation in one list or the other.

2 Labor-management disputes, shareholder voting, and yacht design were given as examples where game theory is useful. Investigate and find some other examples of the use of game theory and report on a particular incident where game theory was used, describing how mathematics affected the situation and the outcome.

Earth Science

Connection 23 Mathematical Models

On October 31, 1983, a group of scientists released a report that made many people seriously reconsider to what extent a nuclear war would affect the planet. Prior to this report it was generally believed that a nuclear war would result in a terrible loss of human life and the destruction of much civilization. The 1983 report suggested that a nuclear war would do far worse damage: it might destroy all life on earth.

The report described a computer simulation on the effects of a nuclear war on the earth's atmosphere. The development of the mathematical model of the earth's atmosphere used in the simulation began long before the report was released. In 1971, the space probe *Mariner 9* was approaching the planet Mars. Telescopic observation indicated that Mars was undergoing huge dust storms. Three scientists, Carl Sagan, O. Brian Toon, and James B. Pollack, developed a mathematical model of Mars' atmosphere and used it in a computer simulation to predict the effect of the dust clouds on Mars' atmosphere. The model was fairly successful in predicting the cooling effects at lower altitudes that *Mariner 9* actually observed.

Pleased with the initial success of their model, the scientists sought to refine it to deal with massive quantities of dust in the earth's atmosphere, such as the dust released by the volcanic eruption of Mount Tambora in Indonesia in 1815. The dust clouds from the eruption affected the earth's weather so severely that 1815 is known as the year of no summer on the eastern seaboard!

In 1980, Luis and Walter Alvarez suggested that dinosaurs became extinct as a result of a comet or an asteroid colliding with the earth. The dust clouds ensuing from the collision caused the earth to cool so rapidly that dinosaurs were exposed to freezing temperatures and the plant life on which they depended died. Toon, Pollack, and another associate, Richard Turco, used this suggestion as an opportunity to further develop and test their *dust-in-the-air* model.

During the late 1970s, a Dutch chemist, Paul Crutzen, carried out research on the effect of smoke on the earth's atmosphere. Crutzen studied the smoke caused by the burning of jungles to obtain farmland. Later, Crutzen was asked to write a paper about the effect of a nuclear war on the earth's ozone layer, which protects the earth's surface from much radiation from space. Crutzen determined that a nuclear war would have little effect on the ozone layer, but his studies on smoke led him to suggest that the smoke from forest fires resulting from a nuclear exchange might be a serious problem.

Turco read Crutzen's suggestion and realized that it provided another opportunity to use the mathematical model he had helped to develop years earlier. A group of scientists, Turco, Toon, Pollack, and Thomas Ackerman, did some preliminary work. Their results led Sagan to rejoin them and together they published the very influential TTAPS report in

October 1983. (TTAPS is an acronym for the names of the report's authors.)

The computer simulation predicted that a nuclear exchange involving only half of the world's arsenal (some 5000 megatons) would send enough dust and smoke into the air to cause a rapid and significant cooling of the earth's surface. Furthermore, the dust could block out enough of the sun's radiation to cause photosynthesis to fail over a major portion of the planet. Plant life would die and the world's food chain would be severed. People who survived the nuclear war would be subject to freezing temperatures, incredibly violent coastal storms, and lack of food.

The model used for TTAPS is recognized to be a preliminary study only. But the results were sufficiently convincing to initiate further computer modelling to study the effects of a nuclear war on the earth's atmosphere. Major refinements to the TTAPS model have suggested that the nuclear winter predicted by the initial study might not be as long or as severe as first thought, but that nuclear winter is a very likely event that would generally add to the havoc resulting from a nuclear war.

Explorations

1. What was the response of politicians to the TTAPS report? What effect do you think the TTAPS report has had on international relations?
2. What were the criticisms of the TTAPS report? How are the limitations of computer simulation related to these criticisms? What do you think were the refinements made to the TTAPS model as a result of the criticisms or advancements in the computer science field?
3. Mathematical models have been used to improve the jumping abilities of Olympics athletes and to reconstruct automobile accident scenarios. Investigate either of these modeling situations or find another that interests you.

Connection 24 Math Models— The Greenhouse Effect

Recently, with the aid of fourth generation "supercomputers" and advances in algorithm development, climatologists have been able to create models which predict possible future changes in the planet's weather patterns. These models are used in developing possible outcomes of the increasing amount of carbon dioxide in our atmosphere.

When fossil fuels such as coal, gasoline, and oil are burned, carbon dioxide is released into the air. Plants absorb carbon dioxide during photosynthesis. But so much of the world's forests have been cut down that significantly less carbon dioxide is being absorbed. The combination of the burning of fossil fuels and the cutting down of forests has resulted in a dramatic, and some climatologists believe, dangerous increase in the amount of atmospheric carbon dioxide.

Carbon dioxide in the air acts like a pane of glass or sheet of plastic in a greenhouse; it allows sunlight to come through, but prevents the resulting heat from escaping. Carbon dioxide allows solar radiation through the atmosphere to the earth's surface, but the earth's ability to cool is reduced because the carbon dioxide traps the heat. This results in a general warming of the earth which has been called the "Greenhouse Effect."

The increase in atmospheric carbon dioxide is an established fact. In 1958, Charles David Keeling of the Scripps Institute of Oceanography established instruments at an altitude of 3.35 km on the Hawaiian volcano, Mauna Loa. By 1984, his measurements indicated a 9.2% increase in carbon dioxide concentration. Keeling's observations have been confirmed by other scientists all over the world. It is anticipated that by 2040 AD the carbon dioxide levels will have doubled.

There is general agreement among climatologists that the increase in carbon dioxide may cause a general warming of the earth and consequently radical changes in the planet's climate. Unfortunately, there is no general agreement on how much of a warming will occur and just exactly what the effects of this warming will be.

If, as some computer simulations suggest, the polar regions warm by 10°C, the polar ice caps will melt and the ocean levels will rise by some 5 meters. This would flood many coastal cities. Weather patterns could change radically, causing the rich farmlands of the continental interiors to become dust bowls. Such arid lands as the Saraha Desert and the Australian interior might well become the farmlands of the next century.

Since 1880 the average surface temperature on the earth has risen by 0.4°C and the ocean levels have risen 12 cm. These changes have been linked in some studies to the Greenhouse Effect. The changes are small, to be sure, but the rate of change seems to be accelerating with the accelerating increase of atmospheric carbon dioxide causing concern among many environmentalists.

Explorations

1. An increase in average temperature for the earth of 0.4°C in 100 years seems very small. What was the change in average temperature during an ice age? Do you think the increase in average temperature in the last century was uniform throughout the world? Give evidence to support your answer.

2. Compare the amounts of CO_2 given off by equal amounts of coal, gasoline, and oil. For the United States, what is the total amount of CO_2 given off by each of these fossil fuels? What suggestions can you make for reducing the amount of CO_2 released into the air?

3. Give an estimate of the amount of CO_2 that your family releases into the air in a year through its use of fossil fuels. Prepare a display which explains how you arrived at your estimate. Compare your results with those of your classmates.

Connection 25 Tides

Tide is the rise and fall of ocean waters on a definite time schedule. All bodies of water, large or small, are subject to the tide-producing forces of the moon. But it is only where oceans and continents meet that tides are noticed; in inland bodies of water the regular rise and fall of the tide is too small to be observed easily. For example, Lake Superior has a tide that rises and falls about 5 cm.

Tides follow the moon in the apparent motion of the moon around the earth. The tides rise and fall twice in the time between two rising moons, which is about 24 hours and 50 minutes. The moon's gravity pulls the water nearest the moon slightly away from the solid part of the earth. At the same time, the moon pulls the solid earth slightly away from the water on the opposite side of the earth. In this way, the moon's gravity produces two bulges on the ocean. These bulges are the positions of high tide. As the earth turns on its axis, the land and water rotate together so that one tidal bulge always stays under the moon, and the other tidal bulge remains on the opposite side to that of the moon. This causes most places on the ocean to have high tide approximately twice a day.

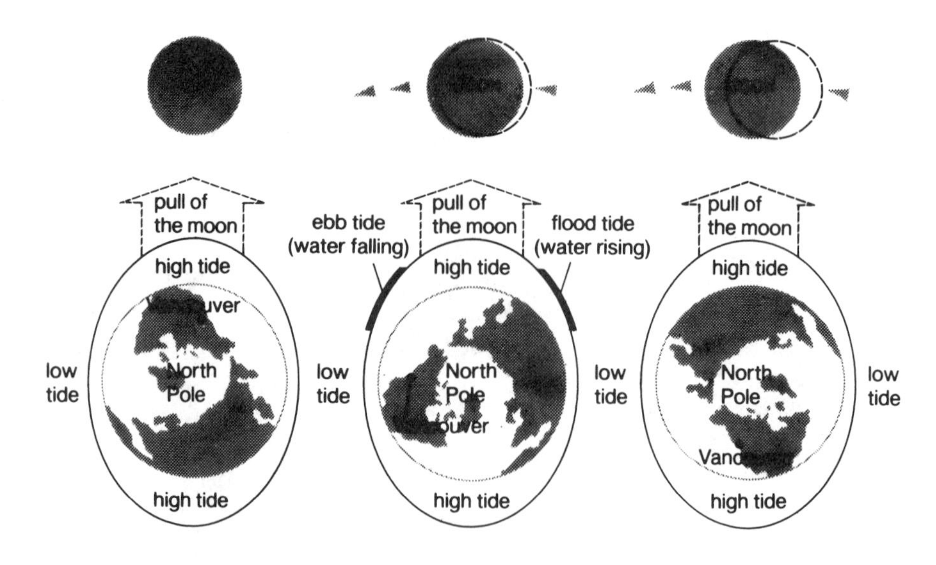

Since there are two high tides in 24 hours and 50 min ($\doteq$ 24.83 h), the rise and fall of the tide is periodic, with a period of approximately $24.83 \div 2 = 12.42$ hours. Thus, the rise and fall of the tides can be modelled mathematically by a sine or cosine function with a period of 12.42 hours.

For example, for equation $y = a \cos kt$, the period is $2\pi \div k$. Thus for tides, $2\pi \div k = 12.42$, which gives $k = 0.51$. Therefore, a tidal equation such as $y = a \cos 0.51t$ gives the height y of the tide when the time t is measured in hours from midnight; a is the height of the water (above sea level) at high tide.

Explorations

1. Consult an atlas or almanac to find out about the heights of tides in various parts of the world. Comment on the variation in height and location of these high tides.

2. Draw a graph of the equation for the height of a tide. Suppose you are sitting on a rock on a bay while the tide is coming in and you can watch the water level rising on the rock. Will the increase in water level be constant or not? If not, when will the increase be fast and when will it be slow? How can the shape of the graph you drew help you to answer these questions?

Connection 26 Waves

Waves that cause destruction on coastlines do so because they have large amounts of energy that they must lose as they break up on shore.

To understand the energy aspect of a wave, consider a wave over water that has a depth h_1 meters. The wave's potential energy (or energy of position) is given by the expression mgh_1 where m represents mass and g is the constant acceleration due to gravity.

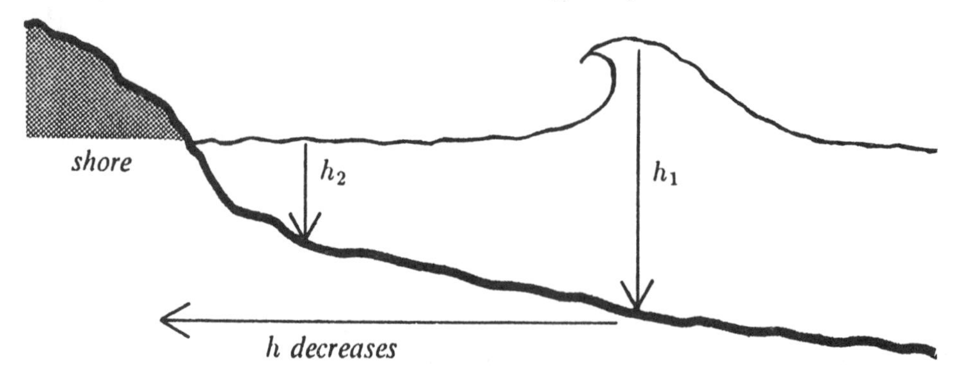

Consider the crest of a wave that is 1 meter in width. If the wave is moving toward shore with a speed of c_1 m/s, then in one second the crest moves c_1 meters. Thus during 1 second, the approximate rectangular volume of water moving toward shore with depth h_1 meters will be $c_1 \times 1 \times h_1 = c_1 h_1 \text{m}^3$. When this wave moves into a shallower depth of h_2 meters, its speed increases to c_2 m/s. This is because the volume $c_2 h_1$ m^3 of water now occupies a rectangular box with volume $c_2 \times 1 \times h_2 = c_2 h_2$ m^3.

That is,

$$c_2 h_2 = c_1 h_1$$

Thus

$$\frac{c_2}{c_1} = \frac{h_1}{h_2}$$

and since

$$\frac{h_1}{h_2} > 1, \quad c_2 > c_1$$

and we see that the speed of the wave increases.

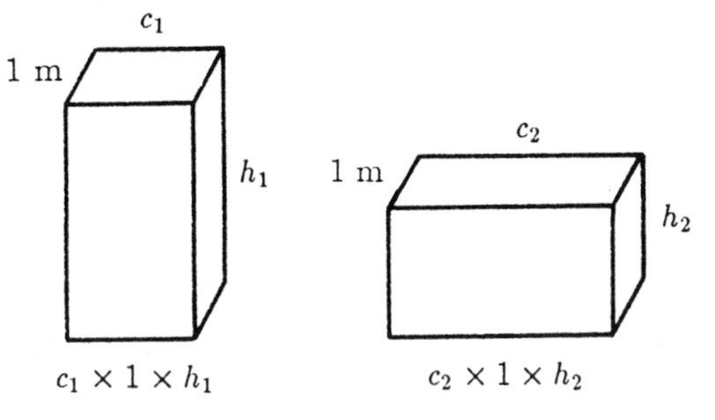

The kinetic energy (or energy of motion) of the wave is given by $\frac{1}{2}mv^2$ where m is mass and v is velocity. In this case, since $c_2 > c_1$, $\frac{1}{2}mc_2^2 > \frac{1}{2}mc_1^2$. We see that the kinetic energy of the water increases as the depth of the water decreases. The increase in kinetic energy is due to the fact that the potential energy of the water has changed to kinetic energy as the water, in effect, falls from a height h_1 to h_2. In fact, this increase in energy equals $mgh_1 - mgh_2$ or $mg(h_1 - h_2)$.

At high tide the heights h_1 are greater than at low tide, so there is more potential energy available to be turned into energy of motion. Thus, other things being equal, the destructive effect of waves, as they lose their energy in breaking up on shore, will be greater at high tide than at low tide.

Mathematical models such as the equation for the energy of a wave help enable scientists to study the effect that ocean waters have on the shoreline.

Explorations

1. Suppose that during high tide at a point offshore where the depth of water is generally 10 meters, the depth increases by 6 meters.
   a) Under normal conditions, what is the change in potential energy for a wave passing from this point to a depth of 1 meter if the mass of the wave is assumed to be 60 kg? Repeat the calculation for the high tide condition.
   b) Using the relationship between potential and kinetic energy, compare the velocities of the waves at the 1 meter depth under the two conditions.

2. Find out what percent of the damage done by recent hurricanes was a result of wave action. Make a chart or graph which shows the relationship between the strength of the hurricane and the amount of damage resulting from wave action. You may want to compare wave damage with other types of damage done by hurricanes.

Connection 27 Food Needs and World Resources

Mathematics is used by economists and social scientists to model the food needs and resources of the entire world. Different people can come to different conclusions using the same information. Thus, it is important for you to understand the statistically based mathematics behind the conclusions you read. The following questions concern food resources and food needs of the world. Answer these questions based on your ideas and beliefs. You can use the statistical information provided to check the validity of your ideas.

Question 1 You are informed almost daily that the world is becoming overpopulated. How much space do all of the people of the world actually occupy?

a) Suppose that each person in the world is enclosed in a thinly walled box so that a person could stand comfortably in it. Then suppose that all of these boxes were placed in a large cube, completely filling it. Which of the following would be closest to the length of the side of this large cube?
A) 1 km B) 10 km C) 100 km D) 1000 km E) 10 000 km

b) Suppose now that each person in the world were given enough space on the ground to stand comfortably as close together as possible but without touching anyone else. If everyone stood inside a square, which of the following numbers would be closest to the length of each side of this square?
A) 10 km B) 20 km C) 100 km D) 1000 km E) 10 000 km

Question 2 Suppose that all of the people of the earth were moved to Canada and placed in a strip 300 km wide immediately north of the United States border. Which of the following numbers multiplied by the population density of Toronto gives a number closest to the population density of this strip across Canada?
A) 0.1 B) 1 C)10 D)100 E)1000

Question 3 You hear about people who are starving not only in third world countries but all over the world. Imagine that you must feed all of the people of the world using only the food that is produced each year in Canada and the United States. Suppose also that you could use only grain and other edible field crops. You are commissioned to divide this food among the whold population of the world so that each person receives the same mass of food daily. Which of the following would be closest to that mass of food?
A) 0.0002 kg B) 0.0002 kg C) 0.02 kg D) 0.2 kg E) 2 kg

Examine the following answers to see how your ideas compare with the facts. The statistics used to obtain the answers are found in the 1987 *World Almanac* and the 1985 *Canada Yearbook.*

Answer 1

a) Assume that a typical person needs a box about 2 m $\times$ 0.5 m $\times$ 0.4 m. The volume of such a box is 0.4 m^3. The population of the world (1985) is 4.8×10^9. Thus the total volume that all of these boxes would occupy is $(4.8 \times 10^9) \times 0.4\ m^3 = 1.92 \times 10^9 m^3 = 1.92\ km^3$. The side of the large box needed to hold this volume would be $\sqrt[3]{1.92} \doteq 1.24$ km.
Thus the correct answer is A.

b) Assume that each person in the world is standing on the ground on a rectangle that is 0.5 m = 0.0005 km wide by 0.4 m = 0.0004 km deep. Thus, each person occupies an area of $0.0005 \times 0.0004\ km^2 = 2 \times 10^{-7} km^2$. The 4.8 billion people of the earth would take up an area of $(2 \times 10^{-7} \times (4.8 \times 10^9) = 9.6 \times 10^2\ km^2$. If this area formed a square the side of the square would be $\sqrt{9.6 \times 10^2} \doteq 31$ km.
The correct answer is B.

Answer 2

The population of metropolitan Toronto (1984) is 2 124 291. The area of metropolitan Toronto is 624 km^2. Thus, the population density of Toronto is $2\,124\,291 \div 624 = 3404$ people per km^2. The distance across Canada from coast to coast is 5187 km. Thus the area of Canada within 300 km of the border of the United States is $5187 \times 300 = 1\,566\,100\ km^2$. Therefore, if the whole world lived in Canada within 300 km of the United States border, the population density within the 300 km wide strip of Canada would be $(4.8 \times 10^9) \div 1\,566\,100 = 3150$ people per km^2. Thus, the correct answer is B.

Answer 3

The figures in the following table are for 1980 to 1984 and give the yield by crop in kilograms.

Crop	Canada	United States
grain	591×10^8	2945×10^8
potatoes	28×10^8	184×10^8
soybeans, pears, beans	12×10^8	134×10^8
other edible field crops	31×10^8	400×10^8
totals	662×10^8	3663×10^8

The total food available each year from Canada and the United States is 4325×10^8 kg. If all of this food were divided among the 4.8 billion inhabitants of the earth, each would receive

$$(4325 \times 10^8) \div (4.8 \times 10^9) \doteq 90 \text{ kg per year}$$

or $90 \div 365 \doteq 0.25$ kg per day. The correct answer is D.

The answers to these questions lead to other questions. Is there any necessity for countries to be overcrowded? Do the people of the world really need to worry about the world being too small? With so much food in Canada and the United States why are there people starving throughout the world? Mathematics cannot answer questions such as these, for they are political and moral questions. But mathematics can help you determine the truth about some of the beliefs you hold and information you are given.

Explorations

1. What factors do you think influence how densely populated an area becomes?

2. Calculate or find the population density of several cities or countries that interest you. Find out how much of the city's or country's land mass is actually habitable. Recalculate the population density omitting the unhabitable land.

3. How much food do you think you consume in one year? Compare your estimate with those of other class members. How much of the food you eat is imported from other countries? Compare the proportion of the world's total food supply produced and consumed by the U.S. with that of another country of your choosing.

Engineering

Connection 28 Ratios for a Reason

The diagram illustrates some parts of a 10-speed bicycle. The following activity will help you discover some interesting ratios between these parts.

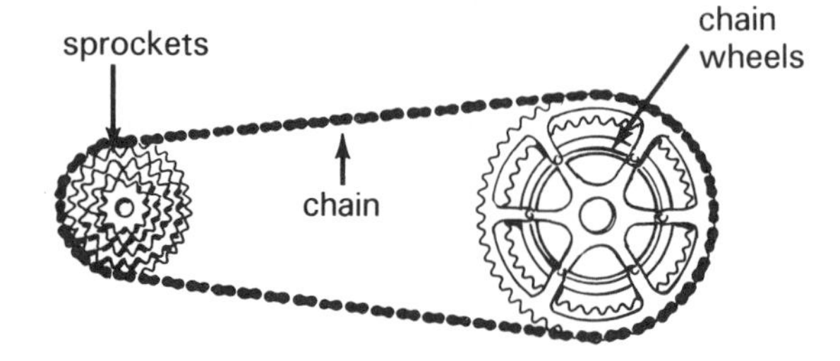

Notice that there are two chain wheels and a number of sprockets in the illustration. The chain encircles only one of the wheels and only one of the sprockets. By changing the position of the chain to another wheel and/or another sprocket, you are changing gear. To investigate the results of changing gears, you will need a 10-speed or 12-speed bicycle, a wooden block, and a piece of chalk. You may want to work with several students to do this activity.

Step 1 Carefully invert the bicycle on its seat and place a wooden block under the handlebars. Make a line on the rear wheel with chalk.

Step 2 Use the pedals to turn the chain wheel one complete rotation. At the same time have someone else count the number of times the rear wheel turns. Repeat this step for each combination of a chain wheel and a sprocket (for example, the largest chain wheel and the second-smallest sprocket; the smallest chain wheel and the smallest sprocket).

Step 3 Record your data in a table. Determine a gear ratio for each combination to compare the number of rear-wheel turns, N, for one turn of the chain wheel.

Chain Wheel	**Sprocket**	**Gear Ratio** $N : 1$
largest	first	:1
·	second	:1
·	·	·
·	·	·
smallest	first	:1
·	second	:1
·	·	·

Step 4 Use your data to answer these questions.

- What combination of chain wheel and sprocket results in the greatest number of rear-wheel turns?
- How would you expect the gear ratio to affect the energy required for pedaling?
- Explain the meaning of *10-speed* in "10-speed bicycle."
- How would you expect a 10-speed bicycle to differ from a 12-speed bicycle?

Explorations

1. Investigate gear ratios in another mechanism such as a clock or a toy. Prepare a chart which illustrates your findings. How do the gear ratios in your mechanism differ from those for the bicycle?

2. By visiting a bicycle shop or obtaining information from a manufacturer, compare gear ratios of several different types of bicycles (for example, a racing bicycle and a cross–country bicycle).

Connection 29 Working with Formulas

You have studied many formulas for finding the volume of a solid. Construction engineers frequently need to use these formulas for their work. For example, they may need to calculate the volume of earth to be removed from a site before construction of the foundation footings of a building, the volume of concrete to be poured into a foundation or a highway, or the number of truckloads of paving material required to complete a stretch of roadway.

$V = \frac{d(a+b)}{2} \times L$

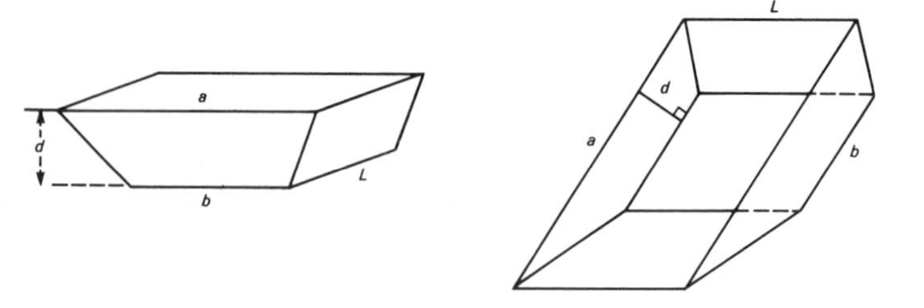

The formula above can be used to calculate the volume of the solids shown. If you know the measurements for d, a, b, and L, you can calculate the volume, V, by substituting directly into the formula. Consider, for example, $d = 6$ m, $a = 62$ m, $b = 41$ m, and $L = 35$ m. The volume is 10 815 m^3.

$$V = \frac{6(62 + 41)}{2} \times 35$$
$$= 10\,815$$

However, the solution is not always as simple to find as the example above. Engineers and scientists frequently have to manipulate the formulas to obtain a solution for a particular variable. For example, if $V = 9165$ m^3, $L = 30.5$ m, $a = 52$ m, and $b = 35.1$ m, how would you calculate the depth, d? Here are two methods.

You could substitute the given measurements into the formula and then solve for d.

$$9165 = \frac{d(52 + 35.1)}{2} \times 30.5$$
$$9165 = 1328.275d$$
$$d = 6.9$$

You could solve the formula for d first and then substitute.

$$2 \times V = \frac{d(a + b)}{\not{2}} \times L \times \not{2}$$

$$\frac{2V}{(a + b) \times L} = \frac{d(a + b) \times \not{L}}{(a + b) \times \not{L}}$$

$$d = \frac{2V}{(a + b) \times L}$$

$$d = \frac{2(9165)}{(52 + 35.1) \times 30.5}$$

$$d = 6.9$$

Explorations

1. Which method would you use if you had to calculate depths for several sets of dimensions? Why?

2. Can you think of an example where engineers would want to know the volume of a sphere in order to do their work? A cylinder?

Connection 30 Construction Electrician

In designing and installing electrical systems, electricians make extensive use of various mathematical formulas. Very frequently these formulas involve radical expressions.

Some of these formulas and their applications are presented in this table.

Formula	Application
$V = \sqrt{PR}$	Calculating voltage in a power circuit with resistance R.
$I = \sqrt{\frac{P}{R}}$	Determining the current in a power circuit.
$Z = \sqrt{X^2 + R^2}$	Finding speaker impedance in a public address system.
$V_T = V_L^2 + V_R^2$	Finding total voltage in an inductive-resistance circuit.
$f_r = \frac{1}{2\pi\sqrt{LC}}$	Calculating resonant frequency of a tuned circuit.

One of the formulas used most frequently is $I = \sqrt{\frac{P}{R}}$. I is current in amperes (A), P is power in watts (W), and R is resistance in ohms (Ω). For a particular circuit, if $P = 1500$ W and $R = 4.6\,\Omega$, then

$$\begin{aligned} I &= \sqrt{\frac{P}{R}} \\ &= \sqrt{\frac{1500}{4.6}} \\ &\doteq \sqrt{326} \\ &= 18 \end{aligned}$$

The current in the circuit is approximately 18 A.

Explorations

1. Investigate one of the other formulas given above and explain how it is used.

2. Invite an electrician or electrical engineer to address your class about mathematical formulas related to electrical work. If you have experience, explain how you have used such formulas.

3. For the formula $I = \sqrt{\frac{P}{R}}$, P is given in watts and R in ohms. If 1 watt = 1 joule/sec and 1 ohm = 1 joule·sec/coulomb^2, what are the units for amperes? You may want to investigate the units for the other formulas in the table.

Connection 31 Trigonometry in Design and Construction

Frequently design and construction projects depend upon the use of trigonometry. This dependence is clearly seen in the construction of a railway tunnel.

Consider the problem of aligning two sections of a tunnel to be constructed through a mountain. The points A and B are fixed survey stations. The given lengths and angles can be measured very accurately using laser technology.

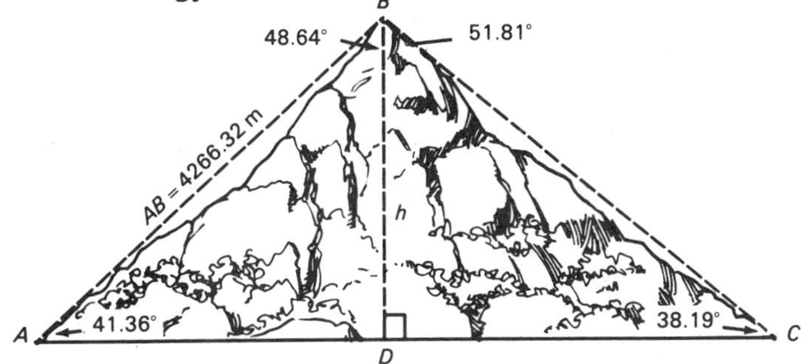

Follow these instructions to determine the position of point C.

Step 1 In $\triangle ABD$ use the given values for the length of AB and the measure of $\angle A$ to calculate the height of the mountain, h, to two decimal places.

Step 2 In $\triangle BCD$ use your calculated value for h, along with the measure of $\angle C$, to calculate the distance BC to two decimal places. When the positions of points A and C and the measures of $\angle A$ and $\angle C$ are known, construction can proceed so that both sections of the tunnel will meet at point D.

What are the advantages of building the tunnel in two separate sections (A to D and C to D) rather than in one section only (A to C)?

Suppose that, through an error in calculation, BC is found to be 4558.15 m. What vertical misalignment would occur at point D?

Explorations

1. Do some research to find out how methods of measurement used in examples like the tunnel problem above have become more accurate.

2. Explain how three other industries or fields of research make use of trigonometry.

3. Find information about two mathematicians who contributed to the development of trigonometry and discuss their contributions.

Space

Connection 32 The Motion of a Free Fall

A very common type of motion is motion with uniform acceleration. An object moving with uniform acceleration changes its velocity (its speed in a certain direction) at a constant rate. This type of motion can be described as follows:

$$\text{acceleration} = \frac{\text{change of velocity}}{\text{time interval}} = \text{constant}$$

$$a = \frac{v_t - v_0}{t} = k,$$ where v_0 is the initial velocity and v_t is the velocity at the end of time interval t.

One of the most common examples of accelerated motion is that of an object allowed to fall freely from a height above the ground. The object falls vertically with increasing velocity and constant acceleration. This constant acceleration is due to gravity and is represented by the symbol g. The value of g has been found to be approximately 9.8 m/s^2.

A ball held at some height above the ground and dropped is an example of free fall. The distance travelled (d) by the ball in time t can be calculated by multiplying t and the average velocity (v) of the ball in time t. Note that the initial velocity of the ball is 0 m/s. The average velocity in time t is given by

$$v = \tfrac{1}{2}(0 + v_t) = \tfrac{1}{2}(9.8)t.$$

Explorations

1. For a uniformly accelerated motion
   a) sketch a velocity-time graph. Represent time on the horizontal axis and velocity on the vertical axis.
   b) sketch an acceleration-time graph with time on the horizontal axis and acceleration on the vertical axis.

2. If a ball is dropped from a building with an initial velocity of 0 m/s,
   a) what is the velocity of the ball after falling 1 s, 2 s, 3 s, and t s?
   b) write and graph the defining equation that relates the velocity (v) of the ball and the time (t).
   c) write and graph the defining equation that relates the distance travelled (d) and the time (t).

3. Galileo and Newton were two sixteenth- and seventeenth-century scientists who made important contributions to our understanding of motion. Research their impact on the development of mathematics and science and report on your findings.

Connection 33 Distortion

If you stand in front of a plane mirror, you will see an image of yourself that is the same shape and size as you are. If you stand in front of a cylindrical curved mirror in a fun house at an amusement park, the image you will see is distorted. The distorted image may be larger or smaller, but it is not the same shape as you are.

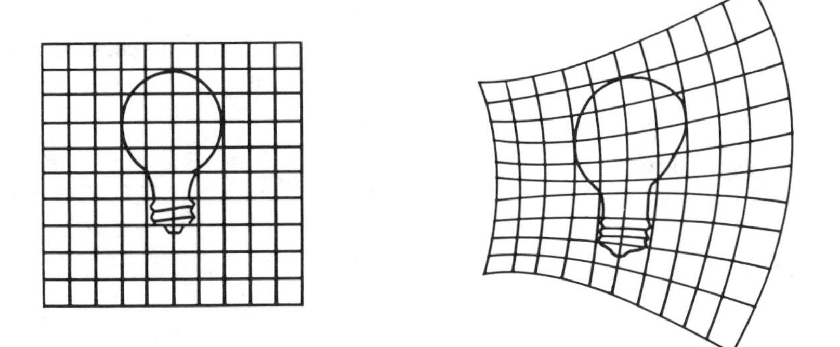

You can draw a figure on regular 10×10 grid paper and obtain a distorted image by copying it onto a distorted 10×10 grid as shown above. You can distort the grid in any way you like as these drawings illustrate.

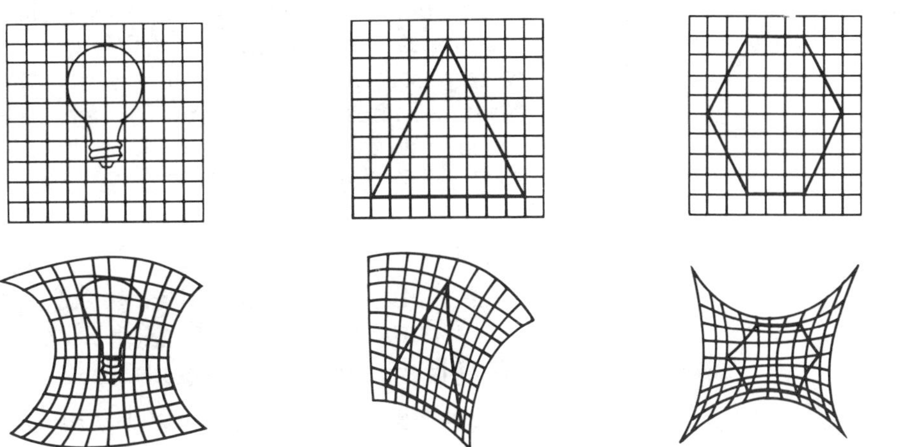

Explorations

1. Make some of your own distortion grids by stretching, curving, and reducing or expanding the axes. How does a distortion differ from a dilatation or expansion?

2. Curved mirrors may also be spherical or parabolic. Find out what kinds of images they produce and some of their important uses.

Connection 34 Black Holes

What exactly is a black hole? A black hole is thought to be a region in space where matter appears to vanish. Scientists believe that when an extremely massive star runs out of nuclear fuel, it begins to collapse under the force of its own gravity. The collapse is very slow at first, but it proceeds with increasing speed. As the star collapses, its volume decreases while its mass remains the same, resulting in an increase in density. In turn, the force of gravity increases tremendously and eventually becomes so intense that even light cannot escape from the star. Since light cannot escape from the star, it appears black.

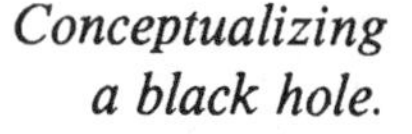

Conceptualizing a black hole.

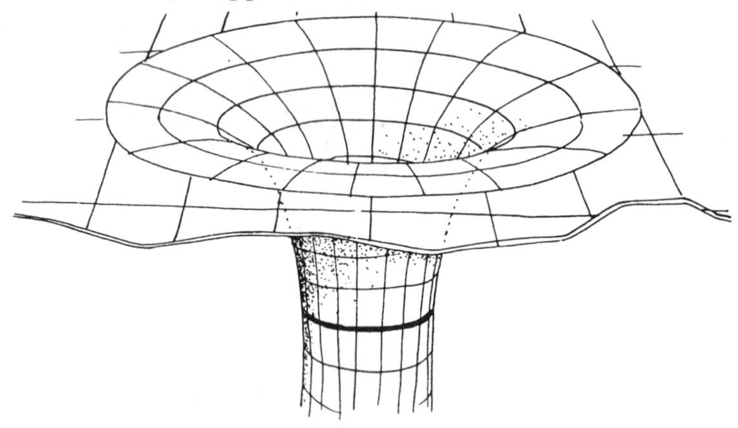

Although the sun is not massive enough to become a black hole, it can be used as an example of how a black hole is formed. The radius of the sun is approximately 700 000 km and its mass is 2×10^{30} kg. If it were possible to compress the sun without changing its mass, it would become increasingly difficult for light to escape from it. When the radius reached a certain critical value, light would not be able to escape at all. This critical value is called the **Schwarzschild radius.**

$$R_s = \frac{2GM}{c^2}$$

R_s is the Schwarzschild radius of the body in meters.
M is the mass of the body in kilograms
G is the gravitational constant, $6.7 \times 10^{-11} \frac{\text{m}^3}{\text{kg} \cdot \text{s}^2}$
c is the speed of light, 3×10^8 m/s.

The Schwarzschild radius of the sun is calculated as follows.

$$R_s = \frac{2 \times 6.7 \times 10^{-11} \times 2 \times 10^{30}}{(3 \times 10^8)^2}$$
$$= 3000 \text{ m}$$

Therefore, if the sun's radius were reduced to 3000 m, or 3 km, theoretically it would become a black hole. The boundary outside this radius is called the **event horizon.** Outside the event horizon it is impossible for an observer to detect what is happening inside, making it extremely difficult to understand how black holes are formed.

Explorations

1. Calculate the Schwarzschild radius for a star the size of Earth.

2. Investigate what happens to a star when it runs out of nuclear fuel.

3. Research the history of theories about black holes. What role did mathematics and mathematicians play?

4. Some scientists have theorized that white holes exist. What are white holes and how are they thought to be related to black holes?

Connection 35 Telescopes

Astronomers face two major problems when they try to study objects in space. The objects, such as stars, quasars, pulsars, and black holes, are at such vast distances from earth that any light, infrared, ultraviolet, radio or other radiation of the electromagnetic spectrum emitted by these objects, is incredibly weak by the time it reaches earth. The second problem astronomers face is that the earth's atmosphere is polluted, which further reduces the strength of the signals reaching earth.

Astronomers tackle the first problem by building signal magnifiers called telescopes. They tackle the second problem by choosing locations for these telescopes very carefully. These locations are far removed from population centers and are at elevations that place the telescopes above most atmospheric pollution.

There are two kinds of telescopes, **refracting telescopes** and **reflecting telescopes**. The earliest telescopes were refractors. Refracting telescopes employ lenses to gather, bend, and focus light and thus make objects appear closer. (See figure 1.) The largest refracting telescope was built in 1897 at Yukes Observatory, Williams Bay, Wisconsin. This telescope measured nearly 19 m in length, with an objective lens approximately 1 m in diameter.

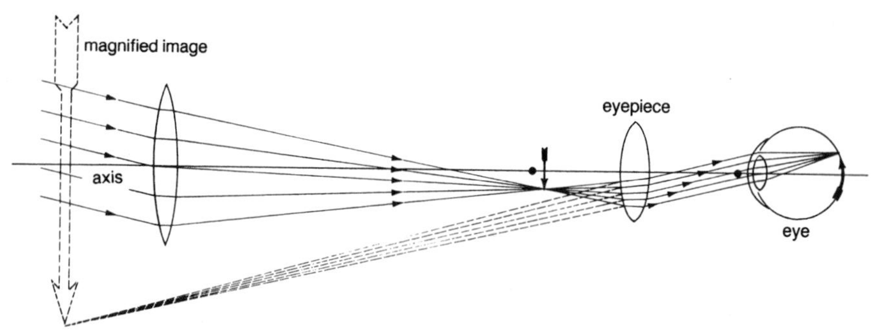

Figure 1
Principle of the refracting telescope.

The largest and most powerful telescopes are reflectors. Reflecting telescopes make use of a parabolic mirror that acts as a radiation collector. The radiation striking the surface of the dish is reflected, by the parabolic property, back through a point in front of the dish, called the focus of the dish. (See figure 2.) It is this focusing of radiation through a point that provides the necessary magnification of the signal.

The largest one-piece, light-reflecting (optical) telescope is situated at an altitude of 2080 m on Mount Semirodriki in the Caucasus Mountains, U.S.S.R. The 6-m mirror of this telescope alone has mass of 70 metric tons. The mass of the whole telescope assembly is 800 metric tons. An even larger reflecting telescope with a 10-m mirror may be found on Mauna Kea, Hawaii. Telescopes of this size are so powerful they can detect light from a candle 24 000 km away! This kind of magnification allows astronomers to see light from objects or events up to 15 billion light years distant, the limit of the observable universe.

As large as optical telescopes are, they are midgets when compared to the giant radio telescopes. Dish radio telescopes operate on the same principle as other reflecting telescopes. The world's largest radio telescope dish is situated in a natural bowl at Arecibo, Puerto Rico. The dish, made up of many separate aluminum plates (as illustrated in figure 2), has a diameter of three football fields.

Figure 2
Principle of the reflecting telescope.

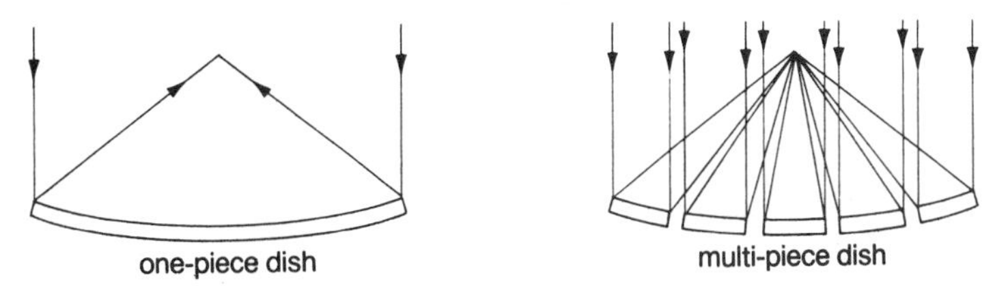

Major improvements in astronomy will take place in space. For example, 1.2 billion dollars are to be spent on an 11-metric ton, 240-cm, NASA reflecting telescope, which is soon to be shuttle-launched into space. Astronomers continue in their efforts to understand our universe and thus to understand our own place in it.

Radio telescopes.

Explorations

1. Do some research on the history of the telescope. When were the first telescopes invented? Who were some of the key inventors? How did increasingly powerful telescopes affect theories of astronomy? Draw a graph which illustrates how the power of the telescope has increased with time.

2. Galileo's observations of the changing positions of the moons of Jupiter had a profound influence on the history of astronomy.
   a) Draw a diagram to illustrate Galileo's observations of the changing positions of the moons of Jupiter.
   b) Find out what Galileo discovered as a result of his observations and explain the role of mathematics in his work.

3. Prepare a chart which shows the size and power of reflecting, refracting, and radio telescopes. Find out how the space telescope will differ in these respects.

Connection 36

Physics and the Geometry of the Universe

During the sixteenth and seventeenth centuries, with the work of such geniuses as Galileo and Sir Isaac Newton, physics took on the scientific form that it has today. One of the key concepts of physics was that of **force**. A force is that which changes the motion of an object.

Newton developed the theory of gravitation as a force. Other physicists developed the theories of electrical and magnetic forces. The work of physicists through the end of the nineteenth century motivated much research work in many areas of mathematics. In one field of mathematics, however, very little change was initiated by the advances of physics: the field of geometry. The geometry developed by the Greek and Hellenic mathematicians many centuries earlier seemed to be a satisfactory mathematical basis for the most sophisticated physical theories.

At the end of the nineteenth and the beginning of the twentieth century, the situation changed dramatically.

James Clerk Maxwell and his peers developed a theory in which a single force, electromagnetism, explained phenomena that previously had to be explained by separate theories of electricity and magnetism. This unifying of forces vastly simplified physical theory.

Albert Einstein, in the Special Theory of Relativity, devised a new theory of gravitation in which effects of gravity were due to the geometry of the universe! The Special Theory stated that the classical geometry of the Greeks was not the true geometry of the universe. Rather, the universe was a four–dimensional structure know as **spacetime**. The presence of mass causes "curves" in spacetime. An object's change in motion due to gravity is caused by the object taking the shortest possible path across the curve in spacetime.

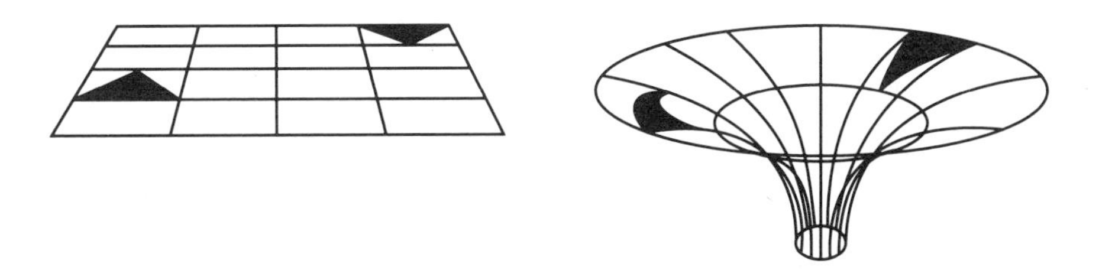

Once the imagination and genius of Albert Einstein had broken away from the classical three–dimensional view of the universe, other creative minds brought forward even more daring ideas.

Theodor Franz Eduard Kaluza, a Russian mathematician, proposed a theory in which the forces of gravity and electromagnetism were described by a single force, in a *five–dimensional* universe! In 1926, the Swedish physicist, Oskar Klein, modified Kaluza's theory so that the discoveries of quantum mechanics were incorporated in this unified force field theory.

The Kaluza-Klein theory, though a remarkable piece of work, was neglected for half a century. One reason for the neglect was that twentieth-century physics used four forces, gravity, electromagnetism, the weak force involved in radioactive decay, and the strong force that holds atomic nuclei together, as its theories. Also, it was very difficult to test the theory by making predictions which could be experimentally verified.

In the late 1960s, due primarily to advances in mathematics, physicists were able to develop what are known as gauge theories which unify electromagnetism with either the weak or strong force. Furthermore, in the 1970s and 1980s there was experimental evidence at high energy accelerator laboratories that supported these theories.

Only gravity had not been successfully integrated into the theories. There was renewed interest among scientists in developing Grand Unification Theories (known as GUT's).

The most recent work suggests that a universe in which all four forces are aspects of a single force (sometimes called "supergravity") has a geometry of *eleven dimensions*! Why eleven? Supergravity theories have been successfully worked out for any number up to eleven, but the theories break down at twelve or more dimensions. So eleven is a maximum. Consider also that seven is the minimum number of dimensions needed to unify the three forces other than gravity. Add these seven dimensions to the four dimensions of Einstein's spacetime and we have eleven again.

How are physicists to refine and confirm their Grand Unification Theories? Some suggest that there is need for new advances in mathematics. To confirm the theories experimentally, some physicists are looking at the biggest laboratory experiment in the universe: the remnants of the Big Bang which physicists believe began the universe some 18 billion years ago.

One thing is for certain: the mathematics of geometry is an exciting and important part of contemporary physics.

Explorations

1. How would you define a dimension? What are the first three dimensions, to which Einstein added time to get the four dimensions of spacetime? Do you think that time is equivalent to length or width? Discuss with your classmates the possibility of a fourth spatial dimension that would be more like the first three.

2. Look out the window with one eye closed. Can you be sure the scene you see is three-dimensional? You probably are aware of depth because you are familiar with the scene, but what if you had never seen it before? Does it make a difference to look with both eyes open? Now move your head from side to side. What clues do you now have about the third dimension? Think about walking around a sculpture (or rotating it). How does point of view influence our perceptions? What equivalent actions can we take to perceive or understand a fourth dimension?

3. Read *Flatland* by Edwin Abbott. Discuss the limitations of seeing the world as two-dimensional instead of three-dimensional. Next think about the limitations of thinking of the world as three-dimensional. Do you see how adding a fourth dimension can be similar to adding a third?

4. The Kaluza-Klein theory is not the only piece of scientific work to be neglected for a long time and then rediscovered. Find other examples.

Connection 37 Non-Euclidean Geometries

Most secondary-school geometry is derived from the geometry that was formulated by Euclid, about 300 B.C. Geometries start with an understanding of certain undefined terms (such as point and line) and an acceptance of certain statements (axioms) without proof.

Euclidean geometry is based on five fundamental axioms.

1) For every two distinct points P, Q, there is a unique line that passes through P and Q.

2) Any line segment $\overline{AB}$ can be extended by a segment $\overline{BE}$ congruent to a given segment $\overline{CD}$.

3) For every point O and every distinct point A, there exists a circle with center O and radius $\overline{OA}$.

4) All right angles are congruent to each other.

The fifth postulate is one that distinguishes Euclidean geometry from the other geometries. Therefore it is referred to by a special name.

5) The Euclidean Parallel Postulate. For every line l and every point P (that does not lie on l), there exists a unique line m from P that is parallel to l.

All of Euclidean geometry can be derived from these axioms. It appears that you can convince yourself that the first four are correct by drawing diagrams. The fifth cannot be verified empirically. (You can never be sure whether a pair of seemingly parallel lines might not indeed meet if you extended them far enough!) For entire centuries, mathematicians tried to prove the fifth axiom from the other four. When direct methods of proof failed, the mathematicians turned to the method of **indirect proof.** This involved assuming that the fifth axiom was false, then proceeding through different stages in the hope that the process would lead to a contradiction. This contradiction would then prove that the fifth axiom must indeed be true.

The startling result was that in doing this, they created new and perfectly consistent (contradiction-free) geometries, with **different** fifth axioms.

Thus there exist three main types of geometry, each of which assumes the truth of the first four axioms. In Euclidean geometry the fifth axiom postulates the existence of a *unique* line (passing through the point P parallel to a given line l that does not contain P). In hyperbolic geometry (developed by Gauss, Bolyai, and Lobachevsky), the fifth axiom postulates the existence of *at least two* distinct lines through P and parallel to l. In elliptic geometry (Hilbert and Riemann) there are *no* parallel lines. All lines perpendicular to the line l meet in one point called the **pole** of l. These different fifth axioms lead to very different properties.

Property	Euclidean	Hyperbolic	Elliptic
A line	is separated into two parts by a point.		is not separated into two parts by a point.
Parallel lines	are equidistant.	are never equidistant.	do not exist.
If a line intersects one of two parallel lines	it must intersect the other.	it may or may not intersect the other.	Parallel lines do not exist.
Two distinct lines perpendicular to the same line	are parallel.		intersect.
The angle sum of a triangle	equals 180°.	< 180°.	> 180°.
The area of a triangle is	independent of its angle sum.	proportional to the difference between its angle sum and 180°.	
Two triangles with equal corresponding angles are	similar.	congruent.	congruent.

At first sight it would appear that many of these results contradict what you observe in the real world. This is because Euclidean geometry is an excellent approximation of reality over relatively short distances (a page of your workbook, the distances measured on a building site, or spaceflights to the moon). When scientists come to measure much larger distances (such as those involved in astronomy) they discover that the geometry of space is *not* Euclidean. Over short distances the analogue of a line is a stretched string. Over large distances a light ray models a line. Scientists have clearly demonstrated that the straight line path of light over astronomical distances is not the straight line of Euclidean geometry, but of Riemann's elliptic geometry.

Einstein used Riemann's ideas of elliptic geometry in his four-dimensional spacetime continuum. Einstein said, "To this (Riemann) interpretation of geometry I attach great importance, for should I have not been acquainted with it, I never would have been able to develop the theory of relativity."

The development of non-Euclidean geometry was an exercise in pure mathematics, which has led to a deeper understanding of our universe.

Explorations

1. Use a globe to check out some properties of hyperbolic geometry. The lines of latitude are parallel lines. Try drawing a triangle on the globe. (You can hold a scrap of paper on the globe and trace the lines onto the paper.) Measure the angles as best you can with a protractor. Is their sum more than or less than 180°? What else can you discover?

2. If a globe approximates a hyperbolic surface, what sort of surface would approximate an elliptic one? Try to make such a surface out of clay or paper. If possible, draw a triangle on the surface and measure the angles as you did above. What are your conclusions?

3. Did Lobachevsky, Gauss, and Bolyai work together to develop hyperbolic geometry? Did Hilbert and Riemann influence each other? See what you can find out about when and where each one worked. Find other times in the history of math or science when several people came up with similar ideas at nearly the same time.

Connection 38 Measurements in Space

Both the United States and the U.S.S.R. use a vast world-wide complex of computers, radars, and communication equipment to track a space vehicle in order to monitor its flight from launch pad to the landing zone. Spacecraft are complex machines. As such they must have a variety of supporting systems, including guidance, navigation, communications, and attitude control, as well as life-support systems. Two-way radio transmission is usually required between ground stations and a space vehicle. Information is telemetered to the ground, and commands are transmitted to the spacecraft to control its mission.

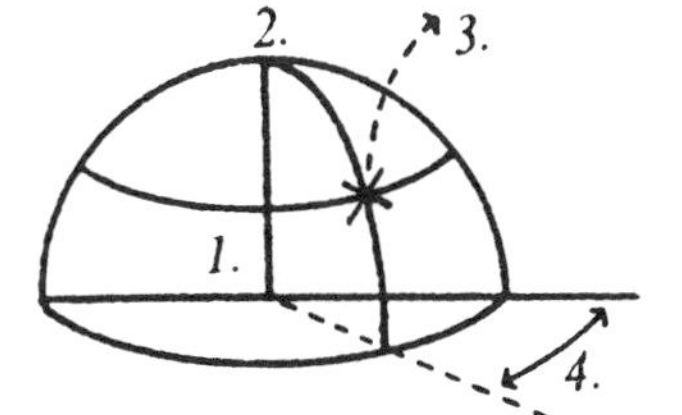

1. observer

2. zenith

3. spacecraft

4. azimuth angle

Early spaceflights were tracked by high-powered radar stations, located around the world so as to maintain continuous radio contact with the spacecraft as the earth rotated. Now, however, communications satellites are also used for this function. Once a launch has been made, information is gathered by the tracking stations and is sent by the space vehicle, to be fed electronically into computers. The information received consists of a continuous stream of "raw data" concerning the speed, position, and performance of the vehicle as well as information about the physical conditions of the astronauts themselves. Computers must accept raw data, compute and deliver results instantaneously and continuously.

Radar tracking of the spacecraft is used to determine the position and velocity of the spacecraft. The position of an object is obtained from a radar set by measuring the elevation and azimuth angles of the radar beam illuminating a target. Measuring the time increment for a signal to make the round trip from the radar antenna to the target and back gives the radial distance to the target. Velocity is measured by the Doppler effect. The return signal is changed in frequency by an amount that is directly proportional to the radial component of the target's velocity. Combined with the other measurements, this last can be used to make accurate computations of speed and direction of motion.

To change a spacecraft's velocity during a flight, both the amount and direction of the velocity adjustment must be controlled. Simple systems employ gyroscopic stabilization of the entire spacecraft by spinning it about its longitudinal axis. The direction having been thus stabilized, only the amount of the velocity needs to be controlled.

More sophisticated attitude control systems employ gyroscopes, star trackers, and computers to control attitude. Very precise accelerometers measure velocity changes. The computer continuously determines the attitude of the spacecraft, based on the gyro's motion. The star trackers detect the position of bright stars whose locations are catalogued in the memory of the computer. The computer uses the apparent position error of the stars to correct for errors accumulated from gyro drift between star sightings. The position of at least two stars must be measured to provide accurate alignment about all three axes of rotation.

From the moment the rocket engines ignite, men, women, and computers monitor the position, the acceleration, the speed, and the direction of the spacecraft, making continuous and informed decisions about the flight.

Explorations

1. Look up the definition of the azimuth angle. How is the azimuth angle used to determine the location of the spacecraft?

2. You are probably familiar with the Doppler effect from hearing the horn of a car or train as it passes by you. What happens to the pitch of the horn as it approaches and then passes you? How does the velocity of the moving car or train affect what you hear?

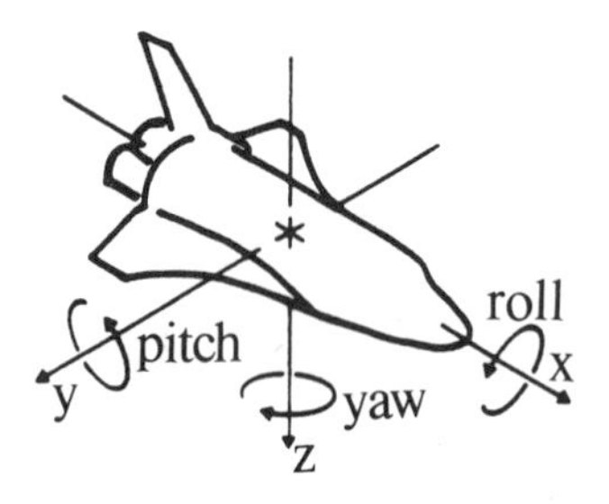

3. Roll, pitch, and yaw of a spaceship are indicated on the diagram. The roll of a spaceship through an angle θ produces a new position of the craft. If you fix the original coordinate grid and set up a moving coordinate system to follow the spaceship's path, then you can describe the new position of a point P on the spaceship after the roll. Let x, y, and z be the coordinates of P on the fixed coordinate system and x', y', and z' be the coordinates of P on the moving coordinate system after the roll. Using your knowledge of trigonometry, develop equations relating x to x', y to y', and z to z'.

Connection 39 Comets (The Cosmic Pinball Machine)

In the late 1940s and early 1950s astronomers proposed a model of the solar system that helped to explain the nature and behavior of comets. Professor Fred Whipple of Harvard University suggested that comets were essentially "dirty iceballs," spheres of frozen material "gluing" together darker, less volatile material. The Dutch astronomer Jan Hendrik Oort hypothesized that the solar system was surrounded by a cloud of these iceballs.

The Oort cloud, as the region of iceballs is known, stretches from just outside the orbit of Pluto to a distance 100 000 times the distance of the earth to the sun. The number of iceballs in the Oort Cloud is believed to be in the trillions!

The solar system and the Oort cloud move through the edges of the Milky Way galaxy in an orbit about the galactic center. As the system moves it comes close enough to neighboring stars so that the gravitational forces "nudge" many of the iceballs from their previous paths. The effect of each nudge is not great. The velocity of an iceball might be changed by some tens of centimeters per second. But the number of iceballs affected by the gravity of nearby stars must be very large, certainly in the tens of millions. The iceballs may be scattered in any direction—some towards the solar system and some away from it.

Of the iceballs moving towards the sun, a few are "nudged" by the gravity of the second largest object in the solar system, the planet Jupiter. These iceballs end up orbiting the sun.

As the iceballs get closer to the sun, the ice in the ball heats up and remarkable things begin to happen. The iceball puts on a sometimes spectacular light show for observers on Earth and earns the name **comet**.

The path followed by these comets was predicted 300 years earlier by the English scientist Sir Isaac Newton. Newton hypothesized that the magnitude of the force of gravity varies inversely as the distance from the object exerting the force. Brilliantly, he deduced that the path of any object orbiting the sun must be an ellipse. The elliptical paths of the planets around the sun are very nearly circular. (Mercury has the least circular orbit of the planets.)

In 1684, Newton communicated his results to another English scientist, Edmond Halley. Halley had been studying comets. At the time it was widely believed that comets described parabolic or hyperbolic paths. A comet travelled close to the sun and then was flung away on a path which would cause it never to return. Halley observed similarities in the paths of comets in 1531, 1607, and again in 1682, and theorized that these three comets might be reappearances of the same comet. Using Newton's idea of an elliptical orbit, Halley was able to "construct" an orbit so that this particular comet should come close to the earth every 76 years. The ellipse of the cometary orbit had a much greater eccentricity (was flatter) than the planetary orbits. This comet is now the most famous of all comets and is known as Halley's comet.

By the time Halley's comet re-approached Earth in 1986, mankind had developed the capability to examine it at closer range. The Soviet Union, the European Space Agency, and Japan each launched space probes to study in detail the composition and nature of the comet. The trajectories of the space probes were carefully plotted so that the probes would enter sun-centered orbits which would intersect the path of Halley's comet at different points.

The information gathered from these probes has kindled renewed interest in comets. Perhaps in 2061, when Halley's comet makes yet another return visit, we will greet it in manned space probes.

Explorations

1. Do you think that Oort's cloud of iceballs is at the edge of the solar system, or do you think that there are other planets beyond Pluto and beyond the Oort cloud? Explain your answer.

2. What is the shape of the Milky Way galaxy? See what you can find out about our solar system's orbit within the Milky Way. For example, how long does it take the solar system to complete an orbit?

3. How did Newton deduce that the path of any object orbiting the sun must be an ellipse? What are the foci of the ellipse? Why do you think Mercury's orbit is the least circular?

4. Are any of the planets orbiting in the same plane? What is the shape of the moon's orbit around the earth? Is its orbit in the same plane as the earth's or not? What do the planes of orbits have to do with eclipses of the sun and moon?

Annotated Bibliography

Albers, D. and Alexanderson, G.L., eds. 1985. *Mathematical People.* Cambridge, MA: Birkhauser Boston, Inc.

Twenty-four candid interviews with some of the most prominent mathematicians of our time, including David Blackwell, Ronald Graham, George Polya, Benoit Mandelbrot, and Olga Taussky-Todd, which provide insight into the motives, philosophies, and talents which drive the creative process.

Bolt, B. 1982. *Mathematical Activities.* Cambridge: Cambridge University Press.

______. 1987. *Even More Mathematical Activities.* Cambridge: Cambridge University Press.

Two collections of puzzles, games, and activities covering a wide range of topics including arithmetic, algebra, geometry, trigonometry, number theory, and game theory.

Copes, W., Sacco, W., Sloyer, C., and Stark, R. 1987. *Contemporary Applied Mathematics Series.* Providence, RI: Janson Publications.

Dynamic Programming

This book is concerned with solving problems in which the "optimal" solution is sought. The solution of these problems involves dynamic programing, a powerful optimization method developed by Richard Bellman. The book begins with straightforward counting and gradually develops more efficient problem-solving techniques formalized in functional form. More complicated examples at the end of the module apply the concepts of permutations and combinations.

Glyphs

Glyphs, or modern picture writing, is becoming increasingly popular as a tool for presenting multi-dimensional data in a meaningful, easy-to-interpret way. This book introduces various types of glyphs and discusses many applications in medicine, astronomy, geology, meteorology, social studies, and sports.

Graph Theory

The objectives of this module are to inform students about the simplicity and utility of graph theory, to provide some of the history of the subject, and to reinforce other mathematical skills. The concepts of chromatic number and planarity are introduced and discussed in-conjunction with the famous Four-Color Conjecture. Trees and directed graphs are introduced while being used in the solution of real problems, some involving the concepts of critical path and slack time.

Mathematics and Medicine

The development and application of indices which measure the severity of patient illness or injury are the topics of interest in this book. Elementary probability and statistical concepts are involved in the solution of these problems.

Queues

This title uses simple algebraic expressions and inequalities to develop solutions for some sample queuing problems. It also illustrates the use of random numbers in simulating additional situations for study.

Information Theory. 1988.

This book introduces information theory, the mathematical treatment of problems that arise with information encoded in binary form. The applications include statellite transmission of data and error correction in compact disc systems. Students apply knowledge of probability, decimal operations, and base 2. Computer projects also included.

Davis, P., and Chinn, W. 1985. *3.1416 and all that.* Cambridge, MA: Birkhauser Boston, Inc.

An entertaining collection of self-contained short essays on topics of current interest. The essays explore the mathematical ideas underlying such topics as prime numbers, the number system, higher dimensions, mathematics and music, linear programming, and geodesics.

Davis, P. and Hersh, R. 1981. *The Mathematical Experience.* Boston: Houghton-Mifflin Company (paperback); Birkhauser Boston, Inc. (hardcover).

A collection of essays about mathematics which conveys the substance of mathematics in discussing its history and philosophy and how mathematical knowledge is elicited.

Kastner, B. 1987. *Space Mathematics.* National Aeronautics and Space Administration, distributed by Dale Seymore Publications, Palo Alto, CA.

A collection of mathematical problems related to space science prepared for use as a supplement in high school courses. It conveys a sense of how secondary school mathematics is actually used by practicing scientists and engineers. Includes problems based on satellites, planets, and space travel. Uses computation and measurement, algebra, geometry, probability and statistics, exponential and logarithmic functions, trigonometry, matrix algebra, conic sections, and calculus.

Perl, T. 1988. *Math Equals.* Meno Park, CA: Addison-Wesley Publishing Company, Inc.

Contains biographies of 9 women mathematicians with mathematical activities relating to the areas where each worked. Introduces students to the kinds of exploration that make mathematics so fascinating to mathematicians. Ten appendices describe key mathematical concepts used in the activities. Bibliography included.

Peterson, I. 1988. *The Mathematical Tourist.* New York: W. H. Freeman & Co. Publishers.

An easy to read book written by a science journalist who is also a former science and mathematics teacher. Peterson introduces the reader to Mathland, a world which includes chaos and order, cryptography and code breaking, labyrinths, higher dimensions, and fractals. Also includes suggestions for further reading.

Petit, J. 1985. *The Adventures of Archibald Higgins.* Providence: Janson Publications, Inc.

A series of witty and informative cartoon books for older students and adults. The lively stories unveil some of the central concepts of modern mathematics and science. Titles which particularly apply here are described below.

The Black Hole

As Archie and his friends consider leaving the universe through a black hole in space, they learn more about geometry in relation to the concepts of space and time.

Everything is Relative

An outing to Cosmic Park gives Archie some insights into questions about time, space, and reality, touching on the fundamentals of physics and Einstein's theory of relativity.

Here's Looking at Euclid

Archie travels to the land of geometry. When he becomes trapped in a quagmire of geometric concepts, Sophie shows up to rescue him with her usual alacrity.

Sloyer, C. 1986. *Fantastiks of Mathematiks.* Providence: Janson Publications, Inc.

Forty lessons that provide a wealth of applications, from epidemics to ecology and medical evaluations to musical scales, that show mathematics really does have a use outside the classroom. The exposition is clear and understandable, supplemented by many graphs and figures. Included are all the step-by-step algebraic manipulations.

Steen, L., ed. 1988. *For All Pratical Purposes.* New York: W.H. Freeman & Co. Inc.

An excellent resource for teachers interested in contemporary mathematics. Includes information on management science, statistics, decision making, patterns and tilings, growth and form, non-Euclidean geometries, and computer science.

Swertka, A. 1987. *Recent Revolutions in Mathematics.* New York: Franklin Watts.

A fascinating look at some recent happenings in mathematics including historical and other background material. Topics include the geometry of Riemann, group theory, probability theory, number theory, fractals, chaos, catastrophe theory, computers, and artificial intelligence. Includes a glossary and bibliography.

Selected Answers

3.2. When the graph has a slope of 1, mass and height are increasing at the same rate. For every cm of height gained, the person also gains one kg of mass.

When the graph is nearly horizontal, the mass is increasing but height is barely increasing. Once people reach adulthood, they often worry about producing such a graph! When the graph is nearly vertical, the height is increasing with only a slight increase in mass. That could happen when someone is growing rapidly but not being properly nourished.

4.2. To estimate the number of terns in the region, use the proportion shown on page 15.

$$\frac{n}{t} \doteq \frac{r}{s}$$

In this case,

$$n = 150$$
$$r = 25$$
$$s = 200$$

We need to find t, the total number of terns.

$$\frac{150}{t} \doteq \frac{25}{200}$$
$$t \doteq 1200$$

5.2. One mathematics text gives the following definition of symmetry:

"A property of a figure that has two or more congruent parts."

A biology book gives this definition:

"The arrangement of organs or other parts of an organism into similar halves around a center or axis."

The biology book also gives examples of two kinds of symmetry, **bilateral** (also called zygomorphic) and **radial** (also called actinomorphic). Mammals have bilateral symmetry; many flowers have radial symmetry.

9.1. June 21, the date of the summer solstice, is the longest day of the year in the northern hemisphere. The sun's path from sunrise to sunset is as long as it can be. At local noon on June 21, the sun reaches the highest point in the sky above the earth that it will reach for each location in the Northern Hemisphere.

At Syene, which is at 23.5° latitude, the sun is directly overhead at noon of June 21. That is why Eratosthenes observed no shadows and saw that deep wells were illuminated by the sun. He could therefore use Syene as a zero point in order to figure out the angle of 7° at Alexandria. He could not have made the same calculations without that zero point; therefore he had to make his observations on June 21.

9.2. Today the circumference of the earth is estimated to be 40 075.16 kilometers at the equator and 40 008.00 km around the poles. Eratosthenes was off by 375 or 308 km or between .7 and .9%.

11.1. The Russell Paradox arises from the concept of a set. A set can either be a member of itself or not. For example, the set of all abstract ideas is itself an abstract idea, but the set of all stars is not itself a star. Suppose we call the set of all sets that are members of themselves M, and the set of all sets that are not members of themselves N. Now the question to consider is this: Is N a member of itself? If N is a member of itself then it must belong to M and then N can't be a member of itself. On the other hand, if N isn't a member of itself then it must belong to N and not M and then it is a member of itself. In either case we have a contradiction. Put in compact notation, if X is any set

$$(X \in N) \leftrightarrow (X \in X)$$

Now let X be N, and we get the contradiction

$$(N \in N) \leftrightarrow (N \notin N)$$

The Russell Paradox is one of many paradoxes discovered in set theory. These paradoxes have raised important questions about logic and the fundamental basis for mathematics.

16.1. We know that

$$x \geqslant 1000$$
$$y \geqslant 1500$$
$$x + y \geqslant 3500$$

We can graph these three inequalities to find the vertices where the minimum values for the inventory cost will occur.

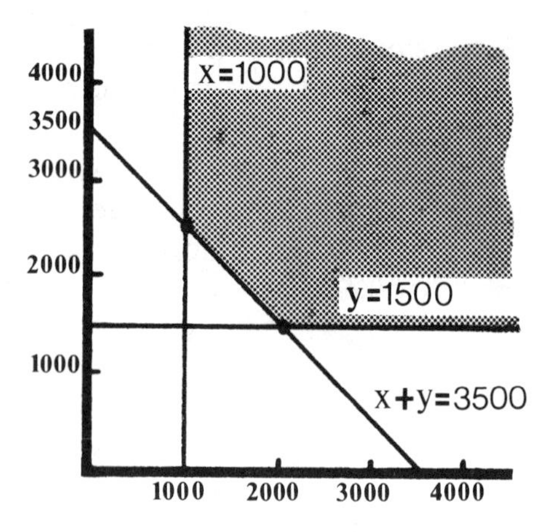

The inventory cost, C, is represented by this equation:

$$C = 5x + 8y$$

At the vertex (1000, 2500), $C = 25\,000$. At the vertex (2000, 1500), $C = 22\,000$). Therefore 22 000 is the minimum inventory cost for Mario Connetti.

18.3–4. Both the amount of storage in computers and the speed of processing data have increased dramatically in the last 30 years. The following graph, reprinted from *Encyclopedia of Science and Technology*, 6th edition, McGraw-Hill, 1987, p. 279, shows the trend for the last 20 years.

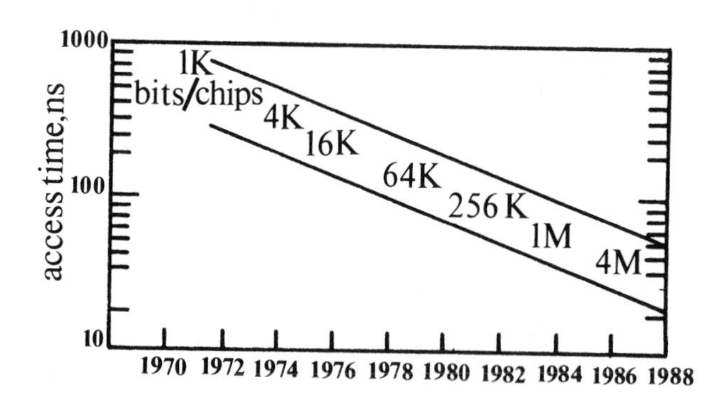

20.2. Prime numbers can end in 3, but not in 5 or 8. Any number (except 5) that ends in 5 will be divisible by 5 and therefore not a prime. Any number ending in 8 is divisible by 2 and therefore not a prime. Many of the first 100 primes can be written in the form $4n + 1$:

$$17 = 4 \times 4 + 1$$
$$29 = 4 \times 7 + 1$$
$$37 = 4 \times 9 + 1$$
$$41 = 4 \times 10 + 1$$

53, 61, 73, 89, 97, 101, 113, 137, etc. can also be written in that form.

21.1. The original message, IN OTHER WORDS, ENGLISH CAN BE WRITTEN MORE COMPACTLY AND STILL BE UNDERSTOOD!, contains 66 characters. The shortened version contains only 46 characters, or 20 fewer characters. The percentage is 20/66 or 30%.

25.2. The graph for the height of a tide over time is that of a cosine function.

The increase in water level is not constant. The rate of increase is greatest about midway between low and high tide. The rate decreases until it is very slight and then zero at the time of the highest tide. The changes in the rate of increase can be seen as the slope of the graph. The slope is steepest between low and high tide and then levels off and is close to zero just before the highest tide. The rate of change is also near zero near the time of lowest tide.

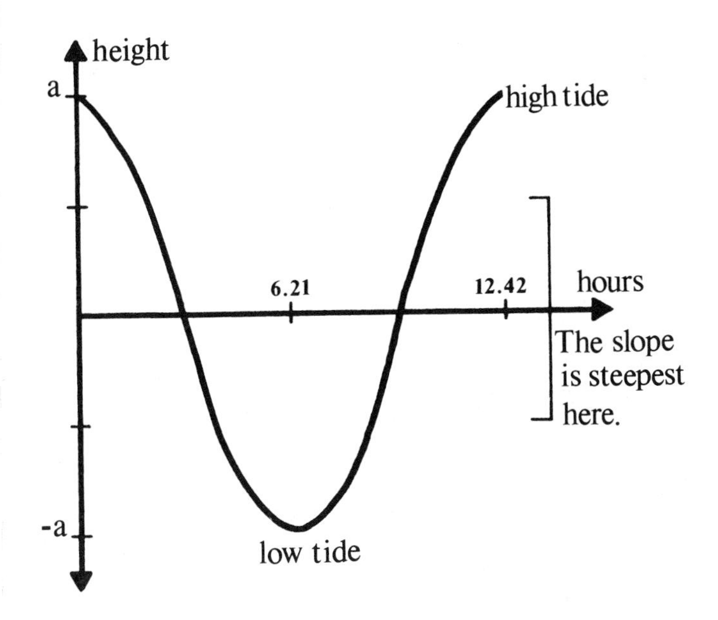

26.1a. Potential energy, PE = mgh. Under normal conditions, the depth is 10 m, so PE = 60 kg × 9.8 m/s² × 10 m.
At a depth of 1 meter, PE = 60 kg ×9.8 m/s² × 1.
The change in potential energy is

$$\begin{aligned} PE_1 - PE_2 &= 60(9.8\ \text{m/s}^2)(10-1) \\ &= 540(9.8\ \text{m/s}^2) \\ &= 5292\frac{\text{kg}\cdot\text{m}^2}{\text{s}^2} \end{aligned}$$

At high tide,

$$\begin{aligned} PE_1 - PE_2 &= 60(9.8\ \text{m/s}^2)(16-1) \\ &= 800(9.8\ \text{m/s}^2) \\ &= 7840\frac{\text{kg}\cdot\text{m}^2}{\text{s}^2} \end{aligned}$$

b. Assuming that kinetic energy is equal to the change in potential energy, at low tide

$$\begin{aligned} KE = \frac{1}{2}60v^2 &= 5292 \\ 30v^2 &= 5292 \\ v^2 &= 176.4 \\ v &\doteq 13.28\ \text{m/s} \end{aligned}$$

At high tide,

$$\begin{aligned} 30v^2 &= 7840 \\ v^2 &= 261.33 \\ v &\doteq 16.17\ \text{m/s} \end{aligned}$$

30.3. To find out the units for amperes, substitute the unit names in the formula, like this:

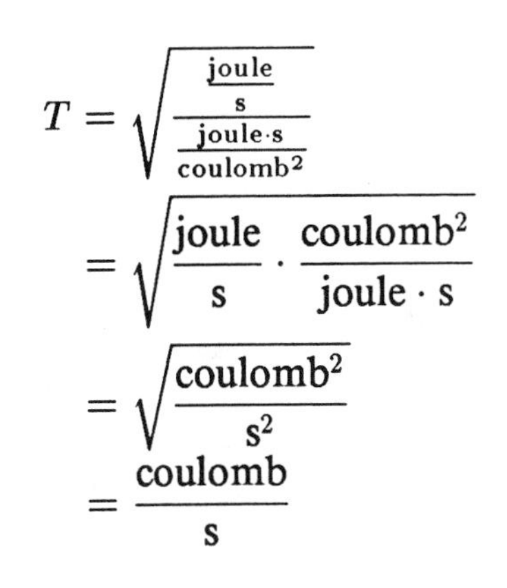

$$\begin{aligned} T &= \sqrt{\frac{\frac{\text{joule}}{\text{s}}}{\frac{\text{joule}\cdot\text{s}}{\text{coulomb}^2}}} \\ &= \sqrt{\frac{\text{joule}}{\text{s}}\cdot\frac{\text{coulomb}^2}{\text{joule}\cdot\text{s}}} \\ &= \sqrt{\frac{\text{coulomb}^2}{\text{s}^2}} \\ &= \frac{\text{coulomb}}{\text{s}} \end{aligned}$$

31. Step 1: To calculate the height of the mountain, h, use the fact that

$$\begin{aligned} \sin A &= h/AB \\ h &= \sin A \times AB \\ h &= \sin 41.36 \times 4266.32 \\ h &= .660788 \times 4266.32 \\ h &= 2819.13 \end{aligned}$$

Step 2: To find the length of BC, use the fact that

$$\begin{aligned} \sin C &= h/BC \\ BC &= h/\sin C \\ BC &= 2819.13/\sin 38.19 \\ BC &= 2819.13/.6182712 \\ BC &= 4459.70 \end{aligned}$$

If BC is found to be 4458.15, then h would be calculated as follows:

$$\begin{aligned} \sin C &= h/BC \\ h &= BC \times \sin C \\ h &= 4458.15 \times .6182712 \\ h &= 2756.35 \end{aligned}$$

But our original calculation for h gave a result of 2819.13. The new result is off by 62.78, and that would be the vertical misalignment at point D.

32.1.

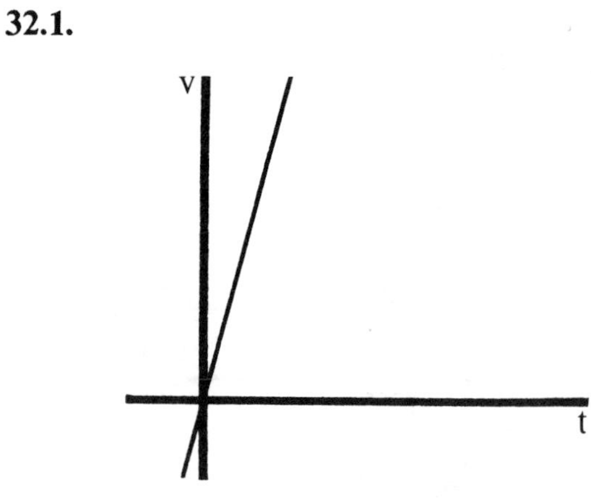

a. velocity
the slope is constant

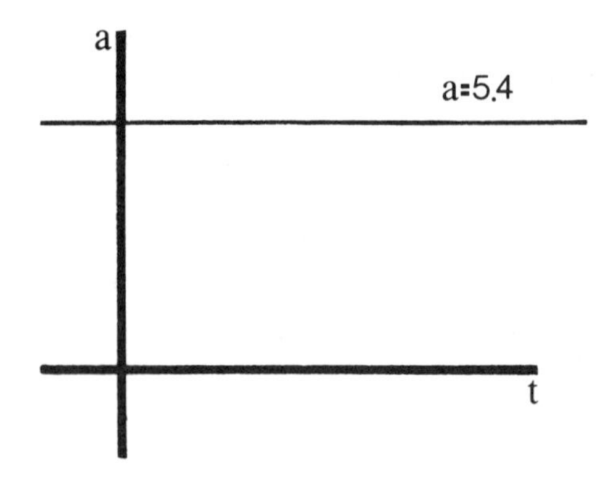

b. acceleration

32.2a. For a ball dropped with an initial velocity of 0 m/s,

$$v_1 = 5.4 \text{ m/s}$$
$$v_2 = 9.8 \text{ m/s}$$
$$v_3 = 16.2 \text{ m/s}$$
$$v_t = 1/2(9.8)t$$

b.

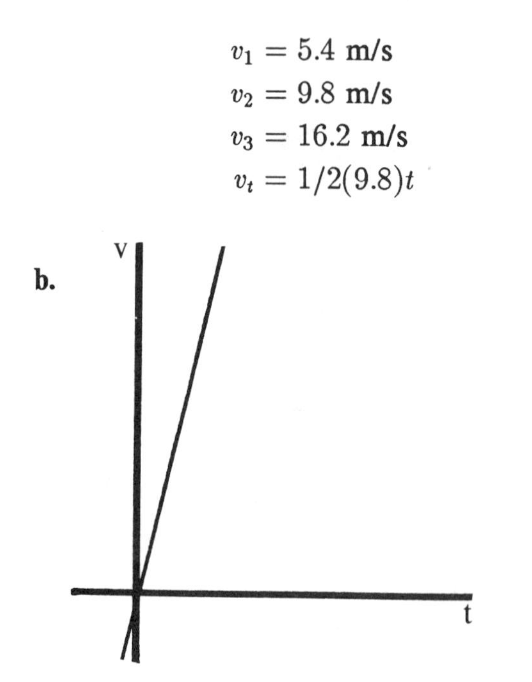

c. Since distance = rate times time,

$$d = \text{velocity}(t)$$
$$d = 1/2(9.8)t(t)$$
$$d = 1/2(9.8)t^2$$

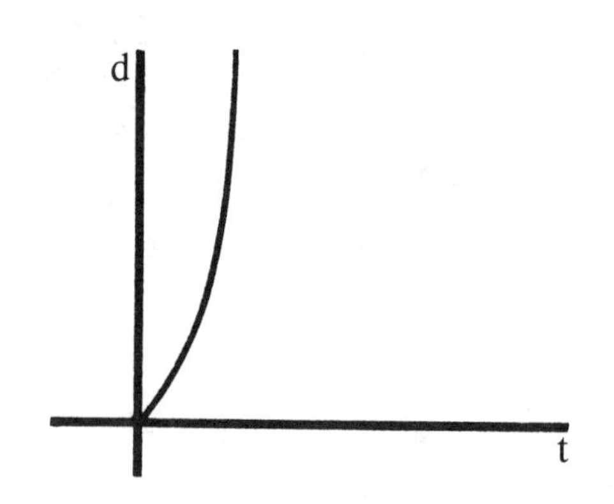

34.1. To calculate the Schwarzschild radius for a star the size of the earth, use the mass of the earth, 6×10^{24} kg.

$$R_s = 2GM/c^2$$
$$= 2 \times 6.7 \times 10^{-11} \times 6 \times 10^{24}/(3 \times 10^8)^2$$
$$= 8.93 \times 10^{-3}$$

35.1. Hans Lippershey of Holland is generally credited with producing the first telescope in 1608. Galileo in 1609 was able to buy a crude telescope and improve upon it. He achieved a magnification of about 33 times. Christiaan Huygens of Holland minimized aberrations by inventing an aerial telescope. James Gregory and Isaac Newton in England developed reflecting telescopes in the 1600's.

35.2. The figure below is an approximate copy of notes made by Galileo on the back of a letter. He recorded the positions of four of Jupiter's satellites from January 14–25, 1611.

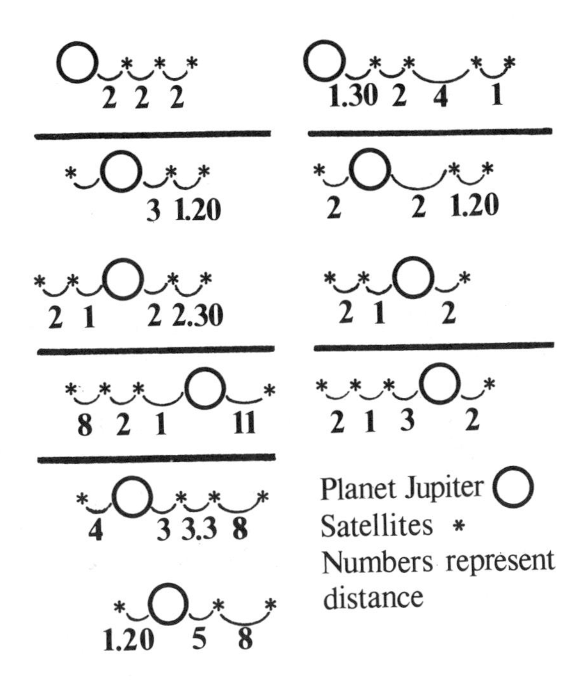

These observations proved that the satellites were revolving around Jupiter. Galileo went on to conclude that the earth and other planets revolve around the sun. Until then it was generally believed that all heavenly bodies revolved around the earth.

36.1. Dimension is any measurable extent. A line is one dimensional and has length; a square or triangle is two dimensional, having length and width. A cube is three dimensional because it has depth as a third dimension. If you think of a cube as an extension of a two-dimensional square into three dimensional space, you can then imagine a hypercube as an extension of a three-dimensional cube into four-dimensional space.

When we look through one eye, we perceive only two dimensions. Sometimes we have to use both eyes, and move around or rotate an object to perceive its depth. Similarly, you might be able to think of looking with new eyes or rotating a hypercube to see its fourth dimension. Thomas Banchoff and his co-workers at Brown University have produced computer graphics which rotate a hypercube and other four-dimensional objects. *The Fourth Dimension: A Guided Tour of the Higher Universes* by Rudy Rucker (Boston: Houghton Mifflin Co, 1984) is a playful and infromative introduction to higher dimensions.

37.3. C.F. Gauss, Janos Bolyai, and Nikolai Lobachevsky are each credited with developing the first non-Euclidean geometry. They did not work together, but they were all influenced by the discussions of the times.

Gauss and Farkas Bolyai (the father of Janos Bolyai) were fellow students at Göttingen University in Germany. They discussed attempts to prove Euclid's parallel postulate from the other postulates. By 1824 Gauss concluded that he could develop a new, consistent geometry based on the denial of the parallel postulate. He did not publish his ideas.

Janos Bolyai as a student in Vienna also discussed Euclid's fifth postulate with a friend and wrote to his father about it. His father told him that he had tried to prove the postulate unsuccessfully and told his son to abandon the attempt. Janos saw that the postulate could be neither proved nor disproved, and his efforts led him to create a non-Euclidean geometry. He published his work as "The Absolute Science of Space" in 1832.

Meanwhile in Russia, Lobachevsky studied under a man who had earlier taught Gauss. Lobachevsky, too, tried and failed to prove Euclid's fifth postulate and was led by that failure to discover a non-Euclidean geometry. He gave an address on the subject in 1826 and published "Elements of Geometry" in 1829–30. His work attracted little notice in Russia and no attention in the rest of Europe because it was written in Russian.

38.1. Because the spacecraft is in three-dimensional space, three measurements must be made to locate it: two angles and a distance. A radar beam illuminates the spacecraft. The angle of elevation and azimuth angle of the beam can be measured. The distance is measured by finding the time needed for a signal to go from the radar antenna to the spacecraft and back.

38.2. As the car or train approaches, the pitch of its horn seems to rise. Then as the object passes by, the pitch seems to drop suddenly. If the object is moving rapidly, the drop in pitch is more pronounced than for a slower object.

38.3. The roll through angle θ is around the x-axis, the forward path of the spaceship, so the x-coordinate of P does not change. Therefore, $x = x'$.

Consider the plane parallel to the y-z plane which contains P. The roll moves P to P' through θ. Let $\angle YOP' = B$ and $r = OP = OP'$. Then, $\angle Y'OP' = B - \theta$. P' has coordinate (y, z) in the fixed reference system, where $y = r\cos B$ and $z = r\sin B$. In the moving spacecraft system, P' has coordinates (y', z'), where $y' = r\cos(B - \theta)$ and $z' = r\sin(B - \theta)$. Expanding the sine and cosine of the difference, we have $y' = r\cos B\cos\theta + r\sin B\sin\theta = y\cos\theta + z\sin\theta$ and $z' = r\sin B\cos\theta - r\cos B\sin\theta = z\cos\theta - y\sin\theta$.

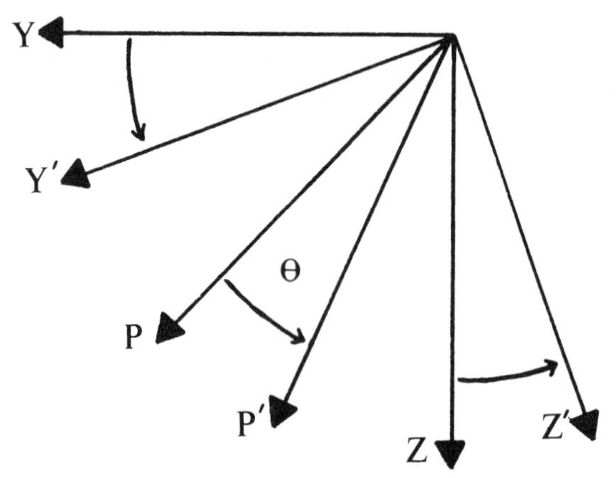

39.2. The Milky Way is shaped like a thin disk with a bulge in the center. Stars, dust, and gases fan out from the central bulge in long, curving arms that form a spiral pattern. Viewed from far above, the Milky Way would resemble a huge, rotating pinwheel. It is classified as a spiral galaxy.

The solar system has a 225 000 000 year period of revolution in the galaxy.

39.3. Most of the planets follow nearly circular paths around the sun with most of the circles nearly in the same plane. Only Mercury and Pluto, the smallest planets, have orbital eccentricities greater than .2 and inclinations great than 5°. (The eccentricity measures departure from circularity, with 0 for a circle and 1 for a parabola. Inclination is the angle between the plane of the plante's orbit and that of the earth.)

Mercury's orbit seems to be perturbed by the gravitational pull of the sun. A small motion of 10' of arc per century was first noticed about 200 years ago. Newton's gravitational theory explained most but not all of the motion. Einstein's general theory of relativity of 1915 explained all of the motion. In fact the motion of Mercury's orbit is considered to be important as an observational verification of Einstein's theory.

39.4. The moon's orbit around the earth is also elliptical. The moon's and earth's orbits are in two different planes. When the moon intersects the plane of the earth's orbit and lies between the sun and the earth, a solar eclipse (eclipse of the sun) results. A lunar eclipse (eclipse of the moon) results when the earth intersects the plane of the moon's orbit and lies between the sun and the moon. The moon is often between the earth and the sun, and the earth is often between the sun and the moon, but an eclipse occurs only when all three are in the same plane.